T0361723

THE OFFICIAL COOKBOOK

By Lisa Kingsley

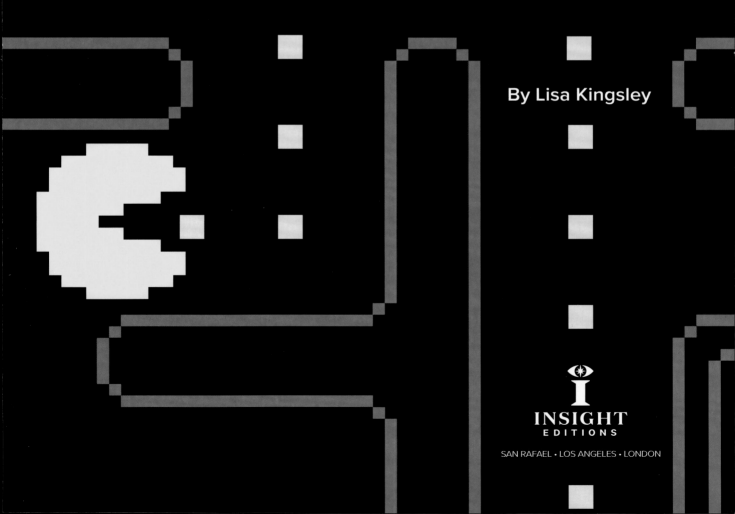

INSIGHT
EDITIONS

SAN RAFAEL • LOS ANGELES • LONDON

CONTENTS

INTRODUCTION

The most popular arcade game of all time started with a pizza.

In the late 1970s, a young video game designer named Tōru Iwatani was working at Namco Limited, a Tokyo-based video game and entertainment company. One day, he looked down at his lunch—a pizza with a slice out—and had the vision of a video game featuring an animated pizza racing around a MAZE eating things. At the time, the budding video game industry was dominated by space-themed shoot-'em-up games that mostly appealed to young men. Iwatani wanted to create a game that would capture a broader audience.

What ultimately became PAC-MAN was a confluence of inspirations. There was the pizza, but Iwatani also drew from Japanese language and culture. The theme of eating became central to the game. There was the children's story about a creature that protected children from MONSTERS (what would become the GHOSTS) by eating them. In kanji—one of three logographic scripts used in Japanese writing—the symbol for "mouth," or kuchi, resembles a parallelogram. Iwatani and his team rounded out the corners, creating a more circular shape to depict PAC-MAN. And then there is the phrase "paku paku," slang for the action of opening and closing one's mouth when eating.

The concept went into production in early 1979, and on May 22, 1980, the CLASSIC game debuted in Japanese arcades as PUCK-MAN. When U.S.-based video game distributor Midway opted to bring it to the United States, it arrived under the name PAC-MAN in October of 1980.

Newfound fans lined up in arcades to try their hand at what seems like a relatively simple concept. The player as PAC-MAN races through a MAZE devouring small PAC-DOTS, larger POWER PELLETS, and FRUITS as a means to accumulate points and move to the next, more challenging level of the game. There's a complication, though. He's chased by four GHOSTS—BLINKY (red), INKY (blue), PINKY (pink), and CLYDE (orange)—each of whom has its own strategy for catching PAC-MAN and gobbling him up. To have your name at the top of the High Score list as PAC-MAN champ was truly a point of pride.

In the years after its American debut, PAC-MAN became a global phenomenon. The first year alone, more than 100,000 game cabinets were sold. By 1990, that number was more than 400,000. PAC-MAN images were licensed and appeared on merchandise of all kinds, more than 500 in all—bicycles, bumper stickers, bed sheets, cereal boxes, T-shirts, and convenience-store cups, to name just a few. AT&T sold a PAC-MAN phone.

The PAC-MAN is included in the permanent collection of the Museum of Modern Art (MoMA) in New York City, and a game cabinet is part of the collection of the Smithsonian Institution in Washington, D.C.

A cultural phenomenon centered on eating is a natural for a cookbook. These PAC-MAN-themed recipes are perfect for munching your way through the day, whether that's breakfast, lunch, dinner, drinks, dessert, or snacks suited for gaming with friends.

Here's to chomping without stopping and hitting your high score! WAKA WAKA WAKA!

ANYONE CAN PLAY—
AND COOK!

There's a well-known adage about PAC-MAN: it's easy to play but hard to master. The same thing can be said about cooking. In both gaming and cooking, the more you do it, the more skills you acquire, and the better you get. All of the recipes in this book are marked with a skill level so you'll know what to expect before you dive in and, in paging through the book, figure out where you want to refine your chops so you can move on to the next level.

Beginner: Even if it's the first time you're grabbing the joystick, you'll have no trouble mastering these recipes. They generally have short ingredients lists, minimal prep, and no special skills required. Instant gratification!

Mid-Level: If you've been around the MAZE a few times, these recipes will present no particular problems for you and will make good use of any kitchen skills you've acquired over time. There may be some tricky turns here and there, but nothing insurmountable.

Pro: These recipes may challenge even the most practiced player, but they definitely have a WOW! factor that's well worth the time and effort. And even if you happen to be a Beginner or Mid-Level player—there's no need to steer clear of them like you do the GHOSTS—they can help you increase your proficiency all the way up to Level 256!

Dietary Considerations
The recipes are also marked with any special dietary considerations that might be important to you:

V+ = Vegan

V = Vegetarian

GF = Gluten Free

DF = Dairy Free

Additionally, by substituting animal proteins with plant-based proteins, wheat flour or products for gluten-free flour or products, and dairy-free products (such as plant-based yogurt, butter, cheese, and milk) for regular dairy products, you can easily customize these recipes to suit your dietary preferences.

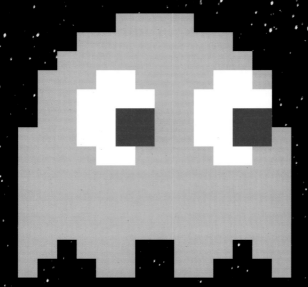

STARTUP
SEQUENCE
BREAKFASTS

Life is a
scramble—get
READY! to bring
your best game with these
recipes that will give you the
energy to navigate the MAZE of your day,
crush all challenges, and take things to
the next level. There's a recipe here for
every taste, situation, and occasion—
from speedy smoothies, to breakfast
bites for on-the-go energy, to
PAC-MAN-inspired pastries
perfect for more leisurely
mornings.

700-POINT APPLE PANCAKE

Mid-Level
V
Active Time: 20 minutes
Total Time: 45 minutes
Makes 4 servings

Up the ante on APPLES! PAC-MAN may not have his choice of APPLES—he seems to like whatever appears in his path—but you can choose. If you like a sweeter APPLE, go with Gala or Fuji. If you like a tart APPLE, opt for green Granny Smith. Either way, this fine FRUIT gets the royal treatment—a quick sauté in butter with brown sugar and cinnamon before being scooped into the center of this puffy oven pancake and topped with maple syrup and powdered sugar.

3 large eggs

½ cup whole milk

½ cup all-purpose flour

2 tablespoons granulated sugar

1 teaspoon lemon zest

½ teaspoon vanilla extract

⅛ teaspoon salt

4 tablespoons unsalted butter, divided

1 medium Gala, Fuji, or Granny Smith APPLE, cored and thinly sliced

3 tablespoons packed brown sugar

¼ teaspoon ground cinnamon

Pure maple syrup

Powdered sugar

1 Preheat the oven to 425°F. In a medium bowl, whisk together the eggs and milk. Add the flour, granulated sugar, lemon zest, vanilla, and salt; whisk until smooth. Let the batter stand for 10 minutes. Stir.

2 In a 10-inch ovenproof skillet, melt 2 tablespoons of the butter over medium-high heat. Remove from the heat. Carefully use a pastry brush to spread the butter up the sides of the skillet. Pour the batter into the center. Transfer to the oven and bake until browned and puffed, about 15 minutes.

3 While the pancake is baking, cook the APPLES in the remaining 2 tablespoons butter in a medium saucepan over medium heat, stirring occasionally, until crisp-tender, about 5 minutes. Add the brown sugar and cinnamon. Cook, stirring occasionally, until the APPLES are tender, 2 to 3 minutes longer.

4 Spoon the APPLES into the center of the pancake. Drizzle lightly with maple syrup and sift powdered sugar on top.

COFFEE-BREAK CAKES

Mid-Level
V
Active Time: 45 minutes
Total Time: 1 hour 35 minutes
Makes 12 cakes

"Coffee Breaks" are brief, humorous interactions between characters that appear between levels of the game. Level up your morning with these tasty cakes—gooey cinnamon rolls that are perfect with a cup of coffee or whatever your preferred a.m. beverage happens to be.

FOR THE FILLING

1 cup brown sugar

2 teaspoons ground cinnamon

¼ cup unsalted butter, melted

1 teaspoon vanilla extract

FOR THE DOUGH

¼ cup warm water (110°F)

4 teaspoons quick-rise yeast

2¾ cups all-purpose flour, plus more for kneading

2 tablespoons granulated sugar

2½ teaspoons baking powder

¾ teaspoon salt

1 cup milk

2 tablespoons unsalted butter, melted

Powdered Sugar Glaze (recipe follows)

1 **Make the filling:** In a small bowl, combine the brown sugar, cinnamon, butter, and vanilla; set aside. Grease twelve 2½-inch muffin cups; set aside.

2 **Make the dough:** In a small bowl, combine the warm water and yeast. Let stand for 5 minutes, until bubbly. In a large mixing bowl, stir together the flour, granulated sugar, baking powder, and salt. Add the milk, yeast mixture, and melted butter, and stir with a wooden spoon until well combined (the mixture will be sticky). Turn out onto a lightly floured surface. Knead in enough flour to make a dough that is not sticky and forms a ball, about 2 minutes.

3 Lightly flour the work surface and roll out the ball of dough to a 12-by-9-inch rectangle. Flour the surface as necessary to prevent sticking. Dollop the filling evenly over the dough and spread to cover the dough, leaving a ½-inch border along one long side. Roll up the dough into a spiral, starting from the long side with the filling. Pinch the edge to seal. With a serrated knife, cut into 12 slices. Place the slices cut-side up in the prepared muffin cups. Let stand in a warm place to rise for 30 minutes.

4 Preheat the oven to 350°F.

5 Bake the cakes until golden brown, 20 to 25 minutes. Let cool in the pan on a wire rack for 5 minutes. Loosen the cakes from the pan with a thin knife or metal spatula. Remove the cakes from the pan. Spread the tops with Powdered Sugar Glaze.

Powdered Sugar Glaze: In a small bowl, combine 1 cup powdered sugar, 1 tablespoon melted butter, 1 teaspoon vanilla extract, and 2 tablespoons milk. Whisk until smooth. Add a little powdered sugar or milk to make the glaze a nice consistency to spoon over the cakes and drip down the sides.

STICKY SITUATION: To help these cakes come out of the muffin cups easier, place little rounds of parchment paper in the bottoms of the greased muffin cups. Peel off the parchment rounds when removing the cakes from the pan.

WARP TUNNEL FUNNEL CAKES

Mid-Level
V
Active Time: 40 minutes
Total Time: 40 minutes
Makes 8 funnel cakes

The WARP TUNNELS let PAC-MAN and his GHOST nemeses travel to the other side of the screen. These lightly sweet and airy pastries will get you to the other side of all kinds of things—hunger, a bad mood, or a bad day.

2 large eggs, at room temperature

1 cup milk

1 cup water

½ teaspoon vanilla extract

3 cups all-purpose flour

¼ cup granulated sugar

1 tablespoon baking powder

¼ teaspoon salt

⅛ teaspoon ground nutmeg

Vegetable oil, for frying

Powdered sugar

1 In a large mixing bowl, beat the eggs lightly to combine. Add the milk, water, and vanilla; whisk until well blended. In another bowl, combine the flour, granulated sugar, baking powder, salt, and nutmeg. Add the milk mixture to the flour mixture. Whisk just until combined; do not overmix.

2 In a deep cast-iron pan or electric skillet, heat 2 to 3 inches of oil to 375°F. Adjust the heat as needed to maintain the temperature while frying. Line two baking sheets with paper towels; set aside.

3 For each cake, cover the bottom of a funnel with your finger; ladle ½ cup of batter into the funnel. Holding the funnel several inches above the oil, release your finger and move the funnel in a square MAZE-like pattern, overlapping in a 4-inch area, until all of the batter is released.

4 Fry until golden brown, about 2 minutes. Turn over with a slotted spoon and fry until golden on the other side, about 2 minutes. Remove to the prepared baking sheets and cool slightly. Repeat with the remaining batter. Sprinkle with powdered sugar.

SUPER SKILLET WITH FRIED EGGS

Beginner
GF, DF
Active Time: 25 minutes
Total Time: 30 minutes
Makes 4 servings

When you need to power up for a really big challenge, fill up on this seriously hearty skillet packed with bacon and sausage, veg, and eggs. Fire it up with a dash of hot sauce!

4 strips bacon, chopped into 1-inch pieces

8 ounces ground pork breakfast sausage

One 10-ounce package frozen diced sweet potatoes

1 small yellow onion, diced

1 large red BELL pepper, seeded and chopped

1 small jalapeño pepper, seeded and diced

2 cloves garlic, minced

1 teaspoon salt

2 cups lightly packed baby kale

2 tablespoons olive oil

4 large eggs

Salt and black pepper

Chopped fresh parsley

1 In a large skillet, cook the bacon over medium heat until crisp, about 5 minutes. Use a slotted spoon to transfer the bacon to a paper towel–lined plate. Drain all but 1 tablespoon of fat from the pan.

2 Cook the pork sausage in the same skillet over medium heat until cooked through, about 5 minutes. Use a slotted spoon to transfer the sausage to a separate paper towel–lined plate. Drain all but 2 tablespoons of fat from the pan.

3 Add the potatoes and onion to the skillet. Cook for 5 minutes over medium heat, stirring occasionally. Add the BELL pepper, jalapeño, garlic, and salt. Cover the pan and cook until the potatoes are tender, 5 to 7 minutes. Add the kale; cook, stirring frequently, until wilted, 3 to 4 minutes. Stir in the cooked sausage.

4 In an extra-large nonstick skillet, heat the oil over medium heat until shimmering. Crack the eggs, one at a time, into a ramekin or small bowl. Carefully slide each egg into the skillet; lightly sprinkle with salt and black pepper. Cook, uncovered, for 1 minute. Cover and cook until the whites are just set and the edges are crisp and golden, about 2 minutes for runny yolks or 2½ minutes for jammy yolks.

5 Divide the hash among four plates. Top with a fried egg, bacon bits, and parsley.

PAC-MAN'S MORNING MILKSHAKE

Beginner
V, GF
Active Time: 10 minutes
Total Time: 10 minutes
Makes 1 serving

Play all day—and start by sipping this delicious smoothie packed with protein from both yogurt and tofu. Silken tofu is the softest style, perfect for blending with other ingredients—you won't even know it's in there!

4 ounces silken tofu

1 small banana, cut into chunks

½ cup vanilla almond milk

½ cup vanilla Greek yogurt

1 cup frozen peaches

1 tablespoon honey

2 or 3 ice cubes (optional)

1 STRAWBERRY, for garnish

1 In a blender, combine the tofu, banana, almond milk, yogurt, peaches, honey, and ice cubes, if using. Blend on low speed, slowly turning up the speed until the blender is on high. Blend until smooth, stopping to stir the mixture if necessary.

2 Pour into a glass and garnish with a STRAWBERRY.

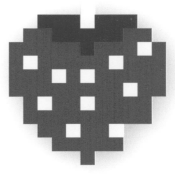

ENERGIZER BREAKFAST BITES

Beginner
V, GF, DF
Active Time: 15 minutes
Total Time: 35 minutes
Makes about 32 cookies

When you need an on-the-go breakfast that will give you a juice boost, grab one of these tasty and nutritious breakfast cookies packed with whole grains, nuts, and dried FRUIT. They'll give you BIG FLASHING DOT energy!

1 cup creamy peanut butter or almond butter

¼ cup honey or pure maple syrup (or 2 tablespoons each)

4 large ripe bananas, mashed

2 large eggs

1 teaspoon vanilla extract

2 cups oat flour

1 cup rolled oats

1 cup chopped walnuts, pecans, and/or almonds

1 cup chopped dried dates or dried CHERRIES

½ cup roasted and salted sunflower seeds or pepitas

1 teaspoon ground cinnamon

1 teaspoon salt

1 teaspoon baking soda

1 Preheat the oven to 350°F. Line two large baking sheets with parchment paper.

2 In a large bowl, stir together the peanut butter, honey, bananas, eggs, and vanilla until smooth.

3 In a medium bowl, stir together the oat flour, oats, nuts, dates, seeds, cinnamon, salt, and baking soda. Add to the peanut butter mixture; stir until well combined. Let stand for 10 minutes.

4 For each cookie, scoop about 2 tablespoons of dough onto the prepared baking sheets 2 inches apart. Bake until set yet slightly soft, 11 to 15 minutes. Let cool on the baking sheets for 5 minutes; transfer to a wire rack to cool completely.

5 Store at room temperature in an airtight container for up to 5 days. Freeze for up to 2 months.

FLOUR POWER: If you can't find oat flour in the supermarket, make your own: Place 2 cups rolled oats in a high-speed blender or food processor. Cover and blend until the oats resemble a fine powder.

GET-OUT-OF-A STRAWBERRY JAM AND BISCUITS

Mid-Level
V
Active Time: 20 minutes
Total Time: 25 hours
Makes 4 or 5 half-pints jam and
10 mini biscuits

These scrumptious PAC-DOT-size biscuits slathered with butter and a super-simple homemade jam will help you escape the peril of hunger and low energy. Take advantage of early summer STRAWBERRIES from a farmers market or pick-your-own berry patch.

FOR THE JAM

4 cups halved fresh ripe STRAWBERRIES

1½ cups sugar

One 1.75-ounce package pectin

¼ cup water

FOR THE BISCUITS

2 cups all-purpose flour, plus more for kneading

1 tablespoon baking powder

1 tablespoon sugar

1 teaspoon salt

6 tablespoons cold unsalted butter

¾ cup buttermilk or whole milk

Melted salted butter

1 Make the jam: In a large bowl, crush the STRAWBERRIES with a potato masher or fork. Press through a fine-mesh strainer into another bowl; reserve the juice for another use. Return the STRAWBERRIES to the large bowl. Add the sugar and stir until combined. Let stand for 10 minutes, stirring occasionally.

2 Meanwhile, in a small saucepan, stir together the pectin and water. Bring to a boil over medium heat, stirring constantly, until the pectin is dissolved and the mixture forms a thick paste, about 1 minute. Add to the STRAWBERRY mixture, stirring constantly, until the sugar is dissolved, 2 to 3 minutes.

3 Fill clean airtight glass jars with the jam, leaving ½ inch of headspace. Seal the lids; let stand at room temperature for 24 hours. Store in the refrigerator for up to 1 month or freeze for up to 1 year.

4 Make the biscuits: Preheat the oven to 425°F. Line a large baking sheet with parchment paper.

5 In a large bowl, stir together the flour, baking powder, sugar, and salt. Use a grater to coarsely shred the butter into the flour mixture. Use a pastry cutter or fork and knife to cut the butter in until the mixture resembles coarse crumbs. Make a well in the center; add the buttermilk, stirring 15 times to just combine (the dough should be sticky).

6 Transfer the dough to a clean well-floured surface. Lightly dust the top with flour and fold the dough in half over itself four times, rotating 90 degrees each time (don't overwork the dough). Use your hands to gently pat the dough to 1 inch thick. Use a floured 1½-inch biscuit cutter to cut out biscuits; place ½ inch apart on the prepared baking sheet.

7 Bake until the tops are lightly golden brown, 10 to 12 minutes. Immediately brush the tops with melted butter. If desired, cut biscuits into PAC-MAN shapes. Serve warm with the STRAWBERRY jam.

EAT EVERYTHING BAGEL BITES

Beginner
V
Active Time: 45 minutes
Total Time: 1 hour 50 minutes
Makes 12 bagel bites

PAC-MAN eats everything in sight! While you can be more discerning, when your bagel flavor options are baffling, go with these fun and easy cream cheese–stuffed bagel bites topped with everything bagel seasoning.

1 pound pizza dough or bread dough, thawed if frozen

4 ounces cream cheese

2 quarts water

2 tablespoons honey

1 tablespoon baking soda

1 egg white beaten with 1 tablespoon water, for egg wash

2 tablespoons everything bagel seasoning

1 Line a large rimmed baking pan with parchment paper. Divide the dough into 12 pieces. Roll each into a smooth ball and place on the prepared pan. Cover loosely with plastic wrap and let stand in a warm place for 30 minutes to rise. Meanwhile, cut the cream cheese into 12 pieces, place on a plate, and freeze.

2 Place an oven rack in the middle of the oven. Preheat the oven to 375°F.

3 Place one of the dough balls on a work surface and gently flatten into a thick disk. Place a piece of frozen cream cheese in the center, then wrap the dough around it to completely encase it. Roll back into a smooth ball and return to the baking pan. Repeat with the remaining dough balls and cream cheese. Cover loosely with plastic wrap and let rise for 15 minutes.

4 In a large pot, combine the water, honey, and baking soda and bring to a boil. Add 3 of the dough balls and boil for 30 seconds. Remove the dough balls from the pot and place on the baking pan. Repeat with the remaining dough balls.

5 Gently brush the dough balls with the egg wash and sprinkle with the everything bagel seasoning.

6 Bake until golden brown, 20 to 25 minutes. Let cool for 15 minutes before serving.

PAC-MAN'S ON-THE-RUN SCRAMBLE WRAPS

Beginner
Active Time: 35 minutes
Total Time: 35 minutes
Makes 4 servings

The scramble is real! For a hot homemade breakfast that will fuel you through any play or workday, grab one of these cheesy egg-meat-veg-stuffed wraps and get after it. They can be frozen and reheated whenever you're READY to dig in.

2 tablespoons olive oil

One 10-ounce package frozen diced sweet potatoes

1 medium yellow onion, diced

1 large red, orange, or yellow BELL pepper, diced

1½ cups lightly packed fresh spinach

1¼ teaspoons salt, divided

¾ teaspoon black pepper

8 large eggs, lightly beaten

⅓ cup milk

4 slices chopped and cooked bacon, ½ cup diced cooked ham, or 8 ounces ground pork sausage, cooked (optional)

1 cup shredded cheddar cheese

Four 12-inch flour tortillas (burrito size)

1 In a large skillet over medium heat, heat the oil until shimmering. Add the potatoes and onion and cook, stirring occasionally, until the potatoes are crisp-tender, about 5 minutes. Add the BELL pepper; cook for 3 minutes. Add the spinach; cook until slightly wilted, about 1 minute. Season with 1 teaspoon of the salt and ½ teaspoon of the black pepper.

2 In a small bowl, whisk together the eggs, milk, remaining ¼ teaspoon salt, and remaining ¼ teaspoon black pepper. Pour the egg mixture over the potato mixture. Cook, without stirring, until the egg begins to set around the edges. Lift and fold the partially cooked egg mixture so the uncooked portion flows underneath. Cook until the egg is cooked through but still moist, 2 to 3 minutes. Add the meat, if using. Sprinkle with the cheese and cook until melted.

3 For each wrap, lay a tortilla on a piece of foil. Spoon one-fourth of the vegetable-egg mixture down the center, leaving 2 inches on each end. Tuck in the sides, then fold the tortilla over the filling and roll closed. Eat immediately or wrap the burritos in the foil and store in an airtight container or resealable plastic bag in the freezer for up to 3 months.

To reheat in an air fryer: Preheat the air fryer to 350°F. Arrange the wraps (in foil) in a single layer in the air fryer basket. Heat for 15 minutes, carefully turning once. Unwrap and serve.

To reheat in the microwave: Remove the foil from one breakfast wrap and wrap in a paper towel. Microwave for 1½ minutes on high power. Turn over and microwave for 1 minute longer. Let stand for 1 minute before serving. Repeat with the remaining wraps.

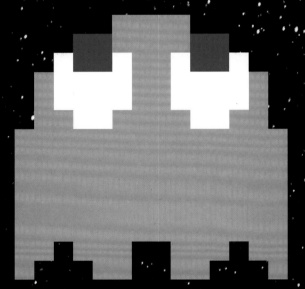

CHAMPION SNACKS

Racing through
the MAZE, running for your
life, while simultaneously
strategizing how to rack up
points can really rev up the appetite.
These awesome snacks—including old-
school arcade-style nachos, crunchy
snack mix, sliders, and pepper poppers—
will let you have one hand maneuvering
the joystick and the other
supplying the munchies to
your mouth.

PAC-DOTS POPCORN

Mid-Level
V, GF
Active Time: 30 minutes
Total Time: 30 minutes
Makes 12 cups

This Parmesan-ranch-seasoned popcorn is not for nibblers! It's for eternally voracious snackers who, like PAC-MAN, can put away 240 popcorn PAC-DOTS before ascending to the next level—only to eat again.

¼ cup freshly grated
Parmesan cheese

2 tablespoons buttermilk powder

½ teaspoon garlic powder

½ teaspoon onion powder

1 teaspoon parsley flakes

¼ teaspoon dried dill

1 teaspoon salt, plus
more as needed

¼ teaspoon finely ground black
pepper, plus more as needed

½ cup unsalted butter

½ cup popcorn kernels

1 In a small food processor or blender, combine the Parmesan cheese, buttermilk powder, garlic powder, onion powder, parsley flakes, dill, salt, and black pepper. Pulse until mixture is a fine powder.

2 Cut the butter into large chunks and melt in a small saucepan on the stove or in a measuring cup in the microwave. Allow to cool slightly while you pop the corn.

3 Pop the corn according to your favorite method (air popper, microwave, stovetop, or electric stirring style). Place the popcorn in a very large bowl. Drizzle the melted butter over all and toss to coat. Sprinkle a little bit of the popcorn seasoning over the popcorn and toss to coat. Continue sprinkling and tossing until either the seasoning has all been used or the popcorn is seasoned to taste. Season with additional salt and pepper, if desired.

4 Serve immediately.

FLOATING GHOST EYES EGG BITES

Beginner
V, DF
Active Time: 30 minutes
Total Time: 1 hour
Makes 16 egg bites

You'll devour these two-bite herbed cream cheese–filled egg bites faster than the floating GHOST eyes can get back to the GHOST HOUSE for rejuvenation and revenge on their constantly consuming adversary.

8 large eggs

One 8-ounce package cream cheese, softened

1 tablespoon milk

2 tablespoons finely grated Parmesan cheese

½ teaspoon onion powder

¼ teaspoon garlic powder

¼ teaspoon salt

1 teaspoon very finely chopped fresh parsley

1 teaspoon very finely chopped fresh dill

1 teaspoon very finely chopped fresh chives

Blue liquid food coloring

1 Place the eggs in a large pot of water to cover. Bring to a boil over medium-high heat. Cover and remove from the heat. Let stand for 12 minutes. Drain and place in a bowl of cool water. When completely cool, peel eggs and cut in half. Scoop the yolks into a bowl; cover, refrigerate, and reserve for another use. Arrange the egg white halves on a serving platter.

2 In a medium bowl, combine the cream cheese, milk, Parmesan cheese, onion powder, garlic powder, and salt. Beat with an electric mixer on medium-high speed until light and fluffy.

3 Add the parsley, dill, and chives and stir well to combine. Add a few drops of blue food coloring until the desired color is achieved. Stir well to combine.

4 Scoop the cream cheese mixture into a small resealable plastic bag. Snip one corner of the bag. Pipe the cream cheese filling into the egg whites. (Or use a pastry bag fitted with a large star tip.)

CHEDDAR CHEESE ARCADE TOKENS

Mid-Level
V
Active Time: 30 minutes
Total Time: 2 hours 45 minutes
Makes about 5 dozen

You've got to pay to play, as they say, but these crisp, buttery cheese coins flavored with dry mustard and cayenne are worth the cheddar. Enjoy with your favorite beverage.

3 cups shredded sharp cheddar cheese

1½ cups all-purpose flour

1 tablespoon cornstarch

1¼ teaspoons dry mustard

1 teaspoon salt

¼ teaspoon cayenne pepper

½ cup cold unsalted butter, cut into ½-inch pieces

3 tablespoons water

Gold luster dust spray (optional)

1. In a food processor, combine cheese, flour, cornstarch, mustard, salt, and cayenne. Process until the mixture is well combined and forms small beads, about 30 seconds.

2. Add one-third of the butter and pulse 5 or 6 times. Repeat twice, until the mixture is the texture of wet sand, stopping to scrape down the sides of the processor as needed. With the processor running, pour the water through the chute, 1 tablespoon at a time, processing just until the dough comes together, 20 to 25 seconds. (Don't overmix—you can lightly knead the dough on a work surface to bring it together into a ball.)

3. Divide the dough in half. Roll each half into a 9- to 10-inch-long log. Wrap the logs tightly in plastic wrap and chill in the refrigerator until firm, at least 1 hour or up to 3 days.

4. Place oven racks in the middle and lower positions. Preheat the oven to 375°F. Line two large rimmed baking pans with parchment paper.

5. Unwrap one dough log and slice crosswise into ¼-inch-thick coins. (Leave the second dough log in the refrigerator while you work with the first one.) You should get about 30 coins from one log. Place 2 inches apart on the prepared pans.

6. Bake until the centers of the cheese coins are set but not crisp and the bottom edges are golden brown and crisp, 14 to 16 minutes, rotating the baking pans between the middle and bottom racks halfway through the baking time. Transfer the coins to a wire rack. Let cool completely. (The cheese coins will continue to crisp up as they cool.)

7. Line the pans with fresh parchment and repeat with the second dough log.

8. If desired, spray coins with luster dust after they have cooled completely.

PEACHY POWER PELLETS

Beginner
V+, GF, DF
Active Time: 15 minutes
Total Time: 15 minutes
Makes 16 servings

Put any kind of challenge in FRIGHT MODE and send it running with these portable, protein-packed energy balls. They'll give you the get-up-and-go to power through even the most daunting day or impossible situation.

1½ cups freeze-dried peaches

½ cup raw almonds

½ cup rolled oats

¼ cup almond butter
or cashew butter

3 tablespoons pure maple syrup

½ teaspoon ground cinnamon

¼ teaspoon ground nutmeg

1 teaspoon vanilla extract

1 Line a large rimmed baking sheet with parchment paper.

2 Add the peaches to a food processor or blender. Cover and pulse or blend to a powder; transfer ¼ cup to a shallow bowl.

3 Add the almonds to the remaining peach powder in the food processor or blender; process or blend until finely ground. Add the oats, almond butter, maple syrup, cinnamon, nutmeg, and vanilla. Process or blend just until combined. If the mixture is dry, add water, 1 teaspoon at a time, until the mixture is sticky.

4 For each POWER PELLET, roll 2 teaspoons of peach mixture into a ball. Roll each ball in the reserved peach powder. Store in an airtight container in the refrigerator for up to 2 weeks or in the freezer for up to 3 months.

CHOMPIN' CHOW

Beginner
V, GF*
Active Time: 15 minutes
Total Time: 15 minutes
Makes 8 cups

You'll enthusiastically chow down on this CLASSIC snack of chocolate- and peanut butter–coated cereal dusted with powdered sugar. Switch up your snack strategy with a few variations: substitute white chocolate for the semisweet and add colorful sprinkles; swap the peanut butter for chocolate hazelnut spread; add pumpkin pie spice; or, after cooling, toss in peanuts, candy, dried FRUIT, mini pretzels, brownie bits, or coconut.

8 cups waffle-shape wheat, rice, and/or corn cereal

1 cup semisweet chocolate chips

½ cup creamy peanut butter

¼ cup unsalted butter

1 teaspoon vanilla extract

1½ cups powdered sugar

1 Add the cereal(s) to a large bowl. In a small saucepan over low heat,** combine the chocolate chips, peanut butter, and butter. Heat, stirring frequently, until melted and smooth. Stir in the vanilla.

2 Pour the chocolate mixture over the cereal; stir until coated. Transfer half of the coated cereal to a large resealable plastic bag. Add half of the powdered sugar. Seal the bag and shake to coat. Spread the mixture on parchment paper. Repeat with the remaining coated cereal and powdered sugar. Let stand until completely cool. Store in an airtight container at room temperature for up to 1 week or in the refrigerator for up to 2 weeks.

*Note: This recipe is gluten free if rice and/or corn cereal is used, but not wheat cereal.

**Tip: Or place the chocolate chips, peanut butter, and butter in a medium glass bowl. Microwave in 30-second intervals until melted and smooth, stirring every 10 seconds.

NOSH-ON SOFT PRETZELS

Mid-Level
V, DF
Active Time: 1 hour
Total Time: 1 hour 45 minutes
Makes 16 large soft pretzels

However you phrase it—eating eternally, chomping without stopping, ingesting infinitely, or noshing on—PAC-MAN is all about it. These big, soft pretzels are the perfect snack for gaming—they require only one hand to hold, there's no messy sauces (just a little yellow mustard), and nothing to spill.

1 tablespoon sugar

One 0.25-ounce envelope active dry yeast (2¼ teaspoons)

2 cups warm water (110°F)

3 cups unbleached bread flour

1 tablespoon kosher salt

1 tablespoon barley malt syrup or honey

2½ to 3 cups all-purpose flour, plus more for kneading

2 quarts water

3 tablespoons baking soda

Coarse kosher salt, for sprinkling

Yellow mustard, for serving

1 In the large bowl of a stand mixer fitted with the paddle attachment, whisk together the sugar, yeast, and warm water. Let stand for 5 minutes or until the yeast is foamy. Add the bread flour, kosher salt, and malt syrup. Mix on low speed to combine. Beat on medium-high speed for 1 minute. (If you don't have a stand mixer, combine ingredients in a large mixing bowl and beat vigorously with a wooden spoon for 3 to 4 minutes.) Stir in as much of the all-purpose flour as you can with a wooden spoon, until dough is quite stiff. Turn out onto a floured surface. Knead briefly until the dough is smooth and elastic. Shape the dough into a ball and place in a clean bowl; cover with plastic wrap and let rise in a warm place until double in size, about 1 hour.

2 Preheat the oven to 450°F. Line two large rimmed baking pans with parchment paper.

3 In a very large pot, combine the water and baking soda. Bring to a simmer. Turn out the risen dough onto a lightly floured surface. Divide the dough evenly into 16 pieces. To make traditional pretzel shapes, roll each portion of dough into a 10-inch rope. Bend the rope into a U shape. Cross the ends and twist them once or twice. Fold the ends over the U shape and press gently to seal. Place the shaped pretzel on the prepared baking pans and repeat shaping the remaining ropes.

4 Place 3 or 4 pretzels at a time in the simmering water bath. Simmer for 1 minute, flipping the pretzels once. Using a slotted spoon, return the pretzels to the baking sheets. As each batch comes out of the water bath, sprinkle generously with coarse kosher salt while still wet. Transfer to the oven and bake for 12 to 15 minutes, or until deep brown colored, rotating the pans once for even browning.

5 Let cool on the pans and then serve with mustard.

INKY'S WINGS

Beginner
GF
Active Time: 20 minutes
Total Time: 40 minutes
Makes 8 servings

It may look like INKY is just flying randomly around, but he's really BLINKY's loyal copilot, moving in tandem with the GHOST GANG leader. Every GHOST has its own singular strategy—BLINKY attacks PAC-MAN when he's within range, PINKY ambushes, and CLYDE is, well, generally less focused. INKY employs all of those schemes. These crispy wings also hit on all cylinders—a little bit sweet, a little bit spicy, crispy, and saucy too.

FOR THE SAUCE

⅔ cup tamari

½ cup sugar

3 tablespoons white distilled vinegar

4 teaspoons finely grated fresh ginger

1 tablespoon unsalted butter

3 cloves garlic, minced

2 teaspoons sesame oil

FOR THE WINGS

4 pounds chicken wings, halved at the joints, wing tips discarded

2 teaspoons garlic powder

1 teaspoon salt

½ teaspoon white pepper

Black and white sesame seeds

3 scallions, sliced on the diagonal

1 Preheat the oven to 400°F. Place a wire cooling rack in a large rimmed baking sheet.

2 Make the sauce: In a medium saucepan over medium heat, stir together the tamari, sugar, vinegar, ginger, butter, garlic, and sesame oil. Cook, stirring frequently, until the sugar is dissolved and the butter is melted, about 2 minutes. Remove from the heat.

3 Make the wings: Pat the chicken dry with paper towels; place in a large bowl. In a small bowl, combine the garlic powder, salt, and pepper; sprinkle over the chicken and toss to coat. Pour half of the sauce over the wings; toss to coat. Arrange the chicken in a single layer on the wire rack.

4 Bake until the chicken is no longer pink, turning once halfway through, 20 to 25 minutes. Use tongs to carefully return the wings to the large bowl. Pour the remaining sauce on top and toss to coat. Transfer to a large serving platter. Sprinkle with sesame seeds and scallions.

Air Fryer Directions: Preheat the air fryer to 400°F. Spray the basket with nonstick cooking spray. In batches, arrange the chicken in the basket in a single layer. Cook until the chicken is no longer pink, turning once halfway through, 18 to 20 minutes. Continue with the recipe as directed above.

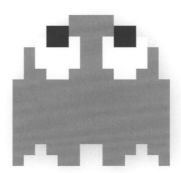

PAC-MAN CHEDDAR-BACON-STUFFED POTATOES

Beginner
GF
Active Time: 30 minutes
Total Time: 1 hour 10 minutes
Makes 8 to 10 servings

PAC-MAN doesn't ever get stuffed, but these twice-baked baby potatoes definitely do—with a sour cream, bacon, butter, and cheese filling. They make a perfect gaming snack or a for-something-different side dish.

16 baby Yukon gold potatoes (about 1½ pounds)

6 slices bacon, finely chopped

2 tablespoons unsalted butter

2 cups finely shredded cheddar cheese

¼ cup sour cream

Salt and black pepper

Olive oil spray

Snipped fresh chives, for garnish

1 Preheat the oven to 400°F. Line two large rimmed baking pans with parchment paper.

2 Pierce the potatoes all over with a fork. Place the potatoes directly on the oven rack and bake until the skins are crispy and the flesh is tender when poked with a fork, 30 to 35 minutes. Transfer the potatoes to a wire rack until cool enough to handle.

3 While the potatoes are baking, cook the bacon in a large skillet over medium-low heat, stirring occasionally, until crisp, 4 to 5 minutes. Using a slotted spoon, transfer the bacon bits to a paper towel–lined plate to drain.

4 When the potatoes are cool enough to handle, slice each potato in half lengthwise. Use a MELON baller or small spoon to scoop the flesh into a bowl, leaving a ¼-inch shell intact. Place the potato skin shells on the prepared baking pans. To the potato flesh in the bowl, add half of the bacon bits, the butter, cheese, sour cream, and a pinch each of salt and pepper. Mash with a fork and mix until well combined. Scoop the mashed potato mixture into the potato shells. Spray lightly with olive oil spray.

5 Bake until the filling is heated through and the topping is golden brown, about 10 minutes.

6 Sprinkle with snipped fresh chives and remaining bacon bits. Serve warm.

CHOCOLATE-DIPPED JOYSTICKS

Beginner
V+, DF
Active Time: 30 minutes
Total Time: 30 minutes
Makes about 30 joysticks

Clutching a joystick promises the rush of the next round of gameplay. Grabbing one of these sweet-salty white chocolate–covered pretzels provokes a different kind of joy, but joy nonetheless.

One 10-ounce package white chocolate melting wafers

½ teaspoon vegetable shortening

One 12-ounce package pretzel rods (about 30)

Candy sprinkles (PAC-MAN colors of blue, yellow, pink, red, and orange)

1 Line a large rimmed baking pan with parchment paper. Place the melting wafers and vegetable shortening in a microwave-safe 9-by-5-inch glass loaf pan. Microwave in 30-second increments, stirring after each interval, until smooth.

2 Arrange single colors of sprinkles in parallel rows on a large flat plate. Holding a pretzel rod at one end, dip in the chocolate, rotating to cover, then pull it out of the chocolate and hold it over the pan, shaking gently, to allow the excess to drip off. Roll the dipped pretzel rods across the rows of sprinkles at a 90-degree angle to create stripes. Place the dipped and decorated pretzel rod on the parchment-lined pan.

3 Repeat with the remaining melted chocolate and candy sprinkles, adding more sprinkles as necessary. Let stand at room temperature until completely set, 30 to 45 minutes.

8-BIT FURIKAKE SNACK MIX

Beginner
V
Active Time: 15 minutes
Total Time: 2 hours 15 minutes
Makes 18 cups

The original PAC-MAN game utilized 8-bit technology to process its images. This crunchy, sweet-and-spicy snack mix has 8 "bites"—ramen noodles, corn cereal, rice cereal, pretzel sticks, fish-shape cheese crackers, oyster crackers, cashews, and wasabi peas—and is powered by furikake, a Japanese seasoning made with dried seaweed (nori), toasted sesame seeds, salt, and various spices. It's CLASSIC!

Three 3-ounce packages ramen noodles

3 cups waffle-shape corn cereal

3 cups waffle-shape rice cereal

2 cups pretzel sticks

2 cups fish-shape cheese crackers

2 cups oyster crackers

2 cups raw cashews

2 cups wasabi peas

½ cup unsalted butter

½ cup light corn syrup

2 tablespoons soy sauce

½ cup furikake seasoning

1 Preheat the oven to 250°F. Line two large rimmed baking sheets with parchment paper.

2 Break up the uncooked ramen noodles and place in a large bowl (reserve the seasoning packets for another use). Add the cereals, pretzels, crackers, cashews, and peas.

3 In a medium saucepan over medium heat, add the butter, corn syrup, and soy sauce and cook, stirring occasionally, until bubbly, 3 to 4 minutes. Pour over the cereal mixture; stir until evenly coated. Sprinkle with the furikake seasoning; stir until combined. Divide between the prepared pans.

4 Bake until lightly toasted, stirring every 15 minutes, about 1 hour. Let stand for 1 hour before serving (the mixture will crisp as it cools).

5 Store in an airtight container for up to 1 week.

NEVER-NIBBLE NACHOS

Beginner
V
Active Time: 10 minutes
Total Time: 15 minutes
Makes 4 servings

When you've been battling GHOSTS for hours and the munchies strike, hit the arcade snack bar for these crunchy nachos covered in homemade queso and topped with spicy, briny pickled jalapeños. PAC-MAN never nibbles, and you won't just graze on these either.

8 cups tortilla chips

2 tablespoons unsalted butter

2 tablespoons all-purpose flour

⅓ cup whole milk

One 1-pound block processed American cheese, cut into 1-inch cubes

Pickled jalapeños, chopped cherry tomatoes, and fresh cilantro

1 Preheat the oven to 350°F.

2 Divide the tortilla chips between two large rimmed baking pans. Bake the chips until warm and crisp, 10 to 15 minutes.

3 Meanwhile, in a medium saucepan over medium heat, melt the butter. Whisk in the flour until combined. Add the milk and stir until slightly thickened. Add the cheese and cook, stirring frequently, until creamy. (If the sauce is too thick to pour, add more milk, 1 tablespoon at a time.)

4 Divide the tortilla chips among four paper boats or plates. Top with the cheese sauce, pickled jalapeños, chopped tomatoes, and cilantro.

BLINKY'S CHILI CHEESE FRIES

Mid-Level
Active Time: 35 minutes
Total Time: 35 minutes
Makes 8 servings

BLINKY's fiery fierceness is the inspiration for these arcade snack bar–style cheese fries topped with seriously spiced chili. If you can't stand the heat, use regular chile powder or 1½ teaspoons of each. And here's a perfectly admissible hack: Swap the homemade cheese sauce for a jar of warmed-up queso.

FOR THE CHILI

1 pound 90% lean ground beef

1 medium onion, diced

3 cloves garlic, minced

One 16-ounce can red kidney beans, drained and rinsed

One 15-ounce can tomato sauce

One 14.5-ounce can fire-roasted diced tomatoes, undrained

½ cup beef broth

One 4-ounce can fire-roasted diced green chiles, drained (optional)

1 tablespoon hot or mild chile powder

1 teaspoon ground cumin

½ teaspoon salt

½ teaspoon black pepper

One 20- to 28-ounce package frozen french fries

FOR THE CHEESE SAUCE

¼ cup unsalted butter

¼ cup all-purpose flour

1½ cups whole milk

One 8-ounce package sharp cheddar cheese, shredded

1 teaspoon onion powder

½ teaspoon garlic powder

½ teaspoon salt

¼ teaspoon black pepper

FOR SERVING

Sour cream

Finely chopped scallions

Hot sauce

1 Preheat the oven to 425°F. Line a large rimmed baking sheet with parchment paper.

2 **Make the chili:** In a large skillet over medium heat, cook the ground beef and onion until the meat is browned, stirring occasionally, 5 to 8 minutes. Drain off the fat. Add the garlic, beans, tomato sauce, diced tomatoes, broth, green chiles, if using, chile powder, cumin, salt, and black pepper. Bring to a boil; lower the heat and simmer, covered, for 20 minutes.

3 Meanwhile, bake the french fries on the prepared baking sheet according to the package directions.

4 **While the fries are baking, make the cheese sauce:** In a medium saucepan over medium heat, melt the butter. Whisk in the flour and cook, whisking constantly, until a thick paste forms. Gradually add the milk, whisking constantly, until the mixture thickens, about 5 minutes. Gradually add the cheese, whisking until completely melted. Whisk in the onion powder, garlic powder, salt, and black pepper. Remove from the heat. (The sauce will continue to thicken as it cools.)

5 To serve, spoon as much of the chili and the cheese sauce over the fries as you'd like. Top with sour cream and scallions. Serve immediately with the hot sauce.

Tip: Refrigerate any leftover chili and cheese sauce in separate airtight containers for up to 5 days.

MAZE MOZZARELLA STICKS

Beginner

V

Active Time: 20 minutes
Total Time: 1 hour 30 minutes
Makes 12 servings

Enjoy these crispy, gooey bites dipped in warm marinara sauce while maneuvering the MAZE. Whatever your strategy—GHOST-chasing and chomping, trapping, or misdirection—they're sure to be a winning snack.

¾ cup all-purpose flour

½ teaspoon salt

½ teaspoon black pepper

2 eggs, lightly beaten

2 tablespoons water

1 cup fine dry Italian-style breadcrumbs

12 mozzarella cheese sticks

Peanut oil, for frying

1 cup marinara sauce, warmed

1 In a shallow dish, combine the flour, salt, and pepper. In another shallow dish, combine the eggs and water. Place the breadcrumbs on a plate. Dip the cheese sticks in the egg mixture, then coat with the flour mixture. Dip the cheese sticks in the eggs again, then roll in the breadcrumbs to coat. Place the coated cheese sticks on a rimmed baking pan. Cover and freeze for 1 hour.

2 Pour about 3 inches of oil into a large pot and heat to 350°F. Add half of the cheese sticks to the pot and fry until crisp and golden, 2 to 3 minutes. Remove to a wire rack set over a baking pan to drain. Fry the remaining cheese sticks, checking to see that the oil temperature is maintained at 350°F before adding them to the pot.

3 Serve the mozzarella sticks with the warm marinara sauce for dipping.

PAC-MAN CHEESE BALL

Beginner
V
Active Time: 30 minutes
Total Time: 1 hour 30 minutes
Makes 12 servings

A CLASSIC game calls for a first-class snack. This retro cheese ball made with cream cheese, cheddar cheese, and bacon and covered with crushed and crunchy cheddar cheese crackers will get gobbled up faster than PAC-MAN hoovers up PAC-DOTS.

FOR THE CHEESE BALL

Two 8-ounce packages cream cheese

One 8-ounce package shredded cheddar cheese

1 tablespoon Worcestershire sauce

½ teaspoon dried thyme

½ teaspoon garlic powder

Few dashes bottled hot pepper sauce

3 slices bacon, crisp-cooked and finely chopped, or ½ cup finely chopped pecans

One 2-ounce jar diced pimientos, drained and patted dry

2 scallions, finely chopped

3 tablespoons chopped fresh chives

1 tablespoon chopped fresh curly-leaf parsley

3 cups square cheddar cheese crackers, finely crushed

Assorted pretzels and crackers

Assorted vegetables for dipping (BELL pepper sticks, cucumber slices, carrot planks, celery sticks, large radish slices)

1 **Make the cheese ball:** Place the cream cheese and cheddar cheese in a large mixing bowl; let stand at room temperature for 30 minutes. Beat the cheeses with an electric mixer on medium speed until nearly smooth, about 3 minutes. Beat in the Worcestershire, thyme, garlic powder, and hot sauce until combined. Add the bacon, pimientos, scallions, chives, and parsley. Beat on low speed until combined.

2 Shape the mixture into a ball. If it is too sticky, chill for 30 minutes. Flatten the ball into a 1¼-inch-thick disk shape. Wrap the disk in plastic wrap and chill for 1 hour or until very firm.

3 Unwrap disk. Use a sharp knife to cut a wedge from the disk to make a PAC-MAN shape. Divide and shape the wedge into 2 small balls. Place the crushed crackers in a pie plate or shallow dish. Place the disk in the crackers and press to stick. Turn the disk over and press the crackers into the other side. Press the crackers onto the sides of disk. Roll the small balls in crackers.

4 Arrange the PAC-MAN-shaped disk on a serving tray along with the small balls. (Alternately, use three square cheese crackers.) Arrange pretzels and vegetable dippers around the cheese. Serve slightly chilled or at room temperature.

MUNCH MIX

Beginner
V+, GF, DF
Active Time: 5 minutes
Total Time: 30 minutes
Makes 5 cups

The name PAC-MAN was partly inspired by the Japanese phrase "paku paku," slang for the action of opening and closing the mouth while eating. These sweet and spicy roasted nuts will definitely get you munching.

2 cups raw whole almonds
and/or walnuts

2 cups raw pecans
and/or cashews

1 cup raw pepitas

3 tablespoons pure maple syrup

2 tablespoons olive oil

1½ teaspoons kosher salt

½ teaspoon Aleppo chile
pepper or cayenne pepper

½ teaspoon vanilla extract

1 Preheat the oven to 325°F. Line a large rimmed baking sheet with parchment paper.

2 In a large bowl, combine the almonds, pecans, and pepitas. In a small bowl, whisk together the maple syrup, oil, salt, chile pepper, and vanilla. Pour over the nuts in the bowl and stir to coat. Spread in a single layer on the prepared baking sheet.

3 Bake, stirring every 10 minutes, until the nuts are golden brown, about 25 minutes. Transfer the pan to a wire rack; let cool completely. Store in an airtight container for up to 2 weeks.

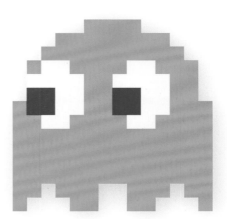

CLYDE'S SLIDERS

Mid-Level
Active Time: 30 minutes
Total Time: 45 minutes
Makes 6 sliders

CLYDE isn't chicken, per se, but he is an endless wanderer. His strategy is generally chasing PAC-MAN to a point, then sliding away and retreating to a corner of the MAZE to hang out and wait for PAC-MAN to come to him. Unlike CLYDE, you won't hesitate to take definitive action on these crisp, breaded chicken patties drizzled with honey and served on homemade flaky biscuits.

FOR THE BISCUITS

2 cups all-purpose flour, plus more for kneading

1 tablespoon baking powder

1 teaspoon salt

6 tablespoons cold unsalted butter

¾ cup buttermilk or whole milk

Salted butter, melted

FOR THE CHICKEN PATTIES

2 large eggs, lightly beaten, divided

¼ cup grated Parmesan cheese

1 cup Italian or plain breadcrumbs, divided

2 scallions, finely chopped

2 cloves garlic, minced

2 teaspoons Worcestershire sauce

¾ teaspoon salt

½ teaspoon smoked paprika or Hungarian paprika

¼ teaspoon black pepper

1 pound ground chicken

½ cup all-purpose flour

4 tablespoons avocado or canola oil

Coarsely shredded iceberg lettuce

Hot honey or regular honey

1 **Make the biscuits:** Preheat the oven to 425°F. Line a large baking sheet with parchment paper.

2 In a large bowl, stir together the flour, baking powder, and salt. Use a grater to coarsely shred the butter into the flour mixture. Use a pastry cutter or fork and knife to cut the butter in until the mixture resembles coarse crumbs. Make a well in the center; add the buttermilk, stirring 15 times to just combine (the dough should be sticky).

3 Transfer the dough to a clean well-floured surface. Lightly dust the top with flour and fold the dough in half over itself four times, rotating 90 degrees each time (don't overwork the dough). Use your hands to gently pat the dough to 1 inch thick. Use a floured 2½-inch biscuit cutter to cut out 6 biscuits; place ½ inch apart on the prepared baking sheet.

4 Bake until the tops are lightly golden brown, 12 to 15 minutes. Immediately brush the tops with melted butter.

5 **Meanwhile, make the chicken patties:** In a medium bowl, stir together one of the eggs, Parmesan cheese, ¼ cup of the breadcrumbs, scallions, garlic, Worcestershire sauce, salt, smoked paprika, and black pepper. Add the chicken; use clean hands to mix until combined. Shape the chicken mixture into 6 balls; use your palm to flatten to ¼ inch thick.

6 Place the flour in one shallow dish, the remaining beaten egg in a second, and the remaining ¾ cup breadcrumbs in a third. Coat both sides of each patty in the flour, then the egg, and lastly the breadcrumbs.

7 In a large skillet, heat 2 tablespoons of the oil over medium heat until shimmering. Add the patties, half at a time, and cook until golden brown on the bottom, 4 to 5 minutes. Flip over and cook until cooked through (165°F), 3 to 5 minutes longer. Repeat with the remaining 2 tablespoons oil and patties. Transfer the patties to a wire rack.

8 Split the biscuits. Top biscuit bottoms with lettuce and chicken patties. Drizzle with honey; add biscuit tops.

Air Fryer Directions: Preheat the air fryer to 380°F. Coat the basket with nonstick cooking spray. Add half of the patties. Cook, turning once halfway through, until golden brown and cooked through (165°F), 10 to 12 minutes.

Make-Ahead Directions: Place uncooked patties in a resealable plastic bag with parchment paper between them and refrigerate for up to 3 days. Freeze uncooked patties in a single layer on a baking sheet lined with parchment paper for 1 hour. Transfer to an airtight container or resealable plastic bag and freeze for up to 3 months. Cook from frozen following the directions above.

PIXEL POPPERS

Beginner
GF
Active Time: 45 minutes
Total Time: 45 minutes
Makes 6 to 8 servings

PAC-MAN travels about 64 pixels per second in his quest to devour as many PAC-DOTS as possible. You'll move faster than that reaching for these scaled-down cream-cheese-and-bacon-stuffed poppers featuring small but mighty shishito peppers. They're sure to illuminate any appetizer spread.

Two 3-ounce packages cream cheese, softened

2 ounces finely shredded cheddar cheese

4 slices cooked bacon, finely crumbled

¼ teaspoon garlic powder

8 ounces shishito peppers

Olive oil spray

Kosher salt

1 Place an oven rack in the upper third of the oven. Preheat the broiler.

2 In a medium bowl, combine the cream cheese, cheddar cheese, bacon, and garlic powder until well mixed.

3 Using a small, sharp knife, make a slit down one side of each of the peppers and scrape out the seeds with a small spoon. Fill the peppers with the cheese mixture, closing the pepper around it. Place cut-side up on a large rimmed baking pan. Coat the peppers lightly with olive oil spray.

4 Broil, turning the pan once from front to back halfway through, until the peppers are starting to char and the cheese is melted, about 4 minutes total. Sprinkle lightly with salt. Serve warm.

CLOSE-CALL MEATBALLS

Beginner
DF
Active Time: 25 minutes
Total Time: 40 minutes
Makes 18 appetizer meatballs

With a GHOST on your tail, you navigate to a POWER PELLET, wait just long enough for the GHOST to almost overtake you, then gobble up the POWER PELLET and the GHOST too. WHEW! Another narrow escape! You get 200 points and a meatball—or two, or three, or four! These Asian-style party meatballs are flavored with soy sauce, ginger, and garlic and served in a spicy, garlicky glaze.

FOR THE SAUCE

1 teaspoon canola or avocado oil

1 medium shallot, thinly sliced

2 teaspoons finely grated fresh ginger

2 cloves garlic, minced

⅓ cup reduced-sodium soy sauce

3 tablespoons rice vinegar

2 tablespoons hoisin sauce

2 teaspoons honey

1 teaspoon sesame oil

½ teaspoon red pepper flakes

FOR THE MEATBALLS

1½ pounds ground turkey breast

¾ cup plain panko breadcrumbs

1 large egg, lightly beaten

2 scallions, finely chopped

2 tablespoons reduced-sodium soy sauce

1 tablespoon finely grated fresh ginger

3 cloves garlic, minced

1 teaspoon salt

½ teaspoon black pepper

FOR GARNISH

Finely chopped scallions

Toasted sesame seeds

1 Preheat the oven to 375°F. Line a large rimmed baking sheet with parchment paper.

2 Make the sauce: In a medium saucepan over medium heat, heat the oil. Add the shallot and cook until tender, about 2 minutes. Add the ginger and garlic; cook for 30 seconds. Remove from the heat. Stir in the soy sauce, vinegar, hoisin sauce, honey, sesame oil, and red pepper flakes. Cover and keep warm.

3 Make the meatballs: In a large bowl, combine the turkey, panko, egg, scallions, soy sauce, ginger, garlic, salt, and black pepper. Use clean hands to mix well. Shape the meat mixture into 18 meatballs; place on the prepared baking sheet.

4 Bake for 15 minutes or until cooked through (165°F). Add the meatballs to the sauce; return to medium heat for 2 minutes. Use a spoon to transfer the meatballs and sauce to a serving platter. Garnish with scallions and sesame seeds. Serve with toothpicks.

A-MAZE-ING
MAIN DISHES

When your goal for the
night is to eat a great dinner
and then spend the rest of it
gobbling up PAC-DOTS, FRUITS, and
frightened GHOSTS, these recipes
have you covered. With arcade snack-
bar CLASSICS, more modern elevated
dishes, plus wildly creative bites,
there's something for every
taste and craving.

BONUS-LIFE BEEF TACO BOWLS

Beginner
Active Time: 30 minutes
Total Time: 45 minutes
Makes 4 servings

Hit 10,000 points and get a Bonus Life! Make the savory ground beef base in this recipe and get three Delicious Dinners! Each recipe calls for 1 pound of the seasoned meat mixture, and you have your choice of beef taco bowls, cheesesteak quesadillas, or cheeseburger pizza. If meat mixture is frozen, thaw overnight in the refrigerator.

FOR THE GROUND BEEF BASE

3 pounds ground beef

1 cup finely chopped carrots

1 cup chopped onion

3 cloves garlic, minced

3 tablespoons tomato paste

2 tablespoons water

1 teaspoon dried Italian seasoning

1 teaspoon salt

½ teaspoon black pepper

FOR THE TACO BOWLS

1 tablespoon chile powder

4 cups hot cooked rice

One 15-ounce can seasoned black beans, heated

2 cups cooked corn kernels

Shredded cheese, salsa, sliced scallions, and sour cream, for topping

1 **Make the ground beef base:** In a large pot over medium-high heat, cook the ground meat, carrots, onion, and garlic until the meat is browned, about 8 minutes. Drain off any fat.

2 In a small bowl, stir together the tomato paste and water. Add tomato paste mixture, Italian seasoning, salt, and pepper to the meat mixture.

3 Divide the mixture into three equal portions. Place two of the portions in two airtight containers or a resealable freezer bag. Store in the refrigerator for up to 3 days or freeze for up to 3 months.

4 **Make the taco bowls:** Return the reserved meat portion to the pot. Add the chile powder and heat until hot.

5 Divide the hot cooked rice among four bowls. Layer on the meat, black beans, and corn. Top with your desired toppings.

Speedy Cheesesteak Quesadillas: In a large skillet over medium heat, heat 1 tablespoon olive oil. Add 3 cups sliced mushrooms, 1¼ cups sliced green pepper, and 1¼ cups thinly sliced onion wedges. Cook until tender, stirring occasionally, about 15 minutes. Transfer the vegetables to a bowl. Add one meat portion to the skillet and heat until hot, stirring occasionally. Place four 10-inch tortillas on a work surface. Top one half of each tortilla with 1 torn slice American cheese or ¼ cup shredded provolone. Top the cheese with the meat and vegetables. Top each with an additional torn slice of American cheese or another ¼ cup shredded provolone. Fold the tortillas in half over the filling. Spray a large nonstick skillet with olive oil spray and heat over medium heat. Add 2 of the quesadillas and cook until golden, about 6 minutes, turning once. Cut into wedges. Repeat with the remaining quesadillas. Drizzle with warmed jarred queso, if desired. Makes 4 servings.

Chompin' Cheeseburger Pizza: Preheat the oven to 425°F. Bring a 1-pound ball of prepared pizza dough to room temperature. Roll into an 11-inch circle and transfer to a 12-inch pizza pan or baking sheet. Prick evenly with a fork. Warm one meat portion in the microwave or in a skillet on the stovetop. Stir together 2 tablespoons ketchup and 2 tablespoons yellow mustard. Spread over the dough. Top with the meat mixture, then with one 8-ounce package shredded cheddar cheese with cream cheese. Bake until the crust is golden and the cheese is melted. Top with ½ cup dill pickle slices and 1 cup shredded lettuce.

USE YOUR NOODLE(S)!

Mid-Level
DF
Active Time: 40 minutes
Total Time: 40 minutes
Makes 2 servings

Achieving PAC-MAN glory involves synthesizing lightning-fast reflexes, strategic thinking, and sharp problem-solving skills. Making this easy ramen-style dish entails combining other things—namely noodles, meat, and veg. Slurping up a big, brothy bowl of it feels every bit as good as hitting your high score.

One 3-ounce package ramen noodles

1 Easy Ramen Egg (recipe follows)

8 ounces pork tenderloin

Salt and black pepper

2 tablespoons vegetable oil, divided

¼ cup sliced scallions, plus more for garnish

1 tablespoon minced fresh ginger

2 cloves garlic, minced

1½ cups chopped or sliced fresh vegetables, such as stemmed shiitake or oyster mushrooms, trimmed snow pea pods, baby bok choy, and/or carrots

2 cups chicken broth

1 tablespoon soy sauce

1 tablespoon rice vinegar

1 teaspoon sriracha sauce (optional)

1 tablespoon white miso stirred together with ¼ cup water

Thinly sliced radish

1 Cook the noodles according to the package directions (reserve the seasoning packet for another use); drain. Rinse with cold water; drain and set aside to cool.

2 Make the Easy Ramen Egg and set aside.

3 Sprinkle the meat with salt and pepper. In a large pot over medium-high heat, heat 1 tablespoon of the oil. Add the meat; cook until slightly pink in the center, stirring frequently, 2 to 4 minutes. Remove from the pot.

4 Add the remaining 1 tablespoon oil, scallions, ginger, and garlic to the pot. Cook and stir over medium heat for 1 minute. Add the vegetables. Cook and stir until the vegetables are crisp-tender, about 3 minutes.

5 Stir in the broth, soy sauce, vinegar, and sriracha, if using. Whisk in the miso mixture. Bring just to a boil. Thinly slice the pork. Stir in the noodles and meat; heat through.

6 Peel and halve the egg. Divide the noodle mixture between two large bowls. Top each with an egg half, radish slices, and additional scallions.

Easy Ramen Eggs: Bring a medium saucepan of water to a boil over medium-high heat. Carefully add desired number of eggs to the water with a slotted spoon. Cook for 6½ minutes on a gentle boil. Transfer to an ice bath and chill until the eggs are slightly warm, about 2 minutes. Gently crack the eggs and peel. Cut in half.

VEGAN VERSION: To make this recipe vegan, substitute 8 ounces firm tofu, sliced into planks. Pat dry and fry in the hot oil until golden brown. Substitute vegan no-chicken broth for the regular chicken broth and omit the egg.

ELEVENTH-LEVEL STUFFED BELL PEPPERS

Beginner
GF
Active Time: 30 minutes
Total Time: 55 minutes
Makes 4 servings

You're 70 points into Level 11, and you're rewarded with a beautiful yellow BELL! You get 3,000 points and the motivation to keep moving! The promise of tucking into these cheesy, tomato-saucy, beef-and-rice-filled BELL peppers will inspire you to get into the kitchen and cook.

4 large yellow BELL peppers

1 pound ground beef, pork, or turkey

1 medium onion, finely chopped

1 clove garlic, minced

Two 15-ounce cans tomato sauce, divided

1 cup shredded Monterey Jack cheese, divided

2 cups cooked rice

½ teaspoon salt

1½ teaspoons chile powder

½ teaspoon smoked paprika

¼ teaspoon dried oregano

Black pepper

1 Preheat the oven to 350°F.

2 Cut off tops from the peppers; remove the seeds and set tops aside.

3 Fill a large bowl with cold water. Bring a large pot of water to a boil over high heat. Cook the pepper "bowls" just until crisp-tender, 3 to 4 minutes. Remove from the pot with kitchen tongs and place in the cold water to stop the cooking process. Drain well and place in an ungreased shallow 3-quart baking dish.

4 In a large skillet over medium heat, cook the beef, onion, and garlic until the beef is no longer pink and the onion is tender, stirring frequently and breaking up the beef with a spoon, 8 to 10 minutes; drain any fat.

5 Stir in 1½ cups of the tomato sauce, ¾ cup of the cheese, the rice, salt, chile powder, smoked paprika, oregano, and black pepper to taste. Spoon into the peppers. Spoon the remaining tomato sauce over the peppers. Bake, along with tops, covered, for 20 minutes. Uncover and sprinkle with the remaining ¼ cup cheese. Bake, uncovered, until tender, 5 to 10 minutes longer.

PAC-MAN PEPPERONI PIE

Mid-Level
Active Time: 45 minutes
Total Time: 1 hour
Makes 4 to 6 servings

Placing a slice of this delicious pepperoni pie into PAC-MAN's legendarily ravenous wedge-shape mouth might just (temporarily) stop his incessant munching, and it will fill you up, too—at least until the hunger hits next.

FOR THE DOUGH

¾ cup warm water (110°F)

1 teaspoon quick-rise yeast

2 cups all-purpose flour, plus more for kneading

½ teaspoon salt

2 tablespoons olive oil, plus more as needed

FOR THE SAUCE

1 tablespoon olive oil

½ cup chopped onion

1 clove garlic, minced

One 14.5-ounce can diced tomatoes

2 teaspoons Italian seasoning blend

1 teaspoon sugar

Salt and black pepper

FOR THE PIZZA

Olive oil, for brushing

Cornmeal

2 ounces sliced pepperoni

4 ounces bocconcini (bite-size) fresh mozzarella balls, halved, or 4 ounces shredded low-moisture mozzarella

Red pepper flakes

1 **Make the dough:** Pour the water into a medium mixing bowl. Sprinkle the yeast over the water; let stand for 5 minutes, until bubbly. Add the flour, salt, and olive oil and stir until combined. Turn out the dough onto a lightly floured surface. Shape into a ball and gently knead in more flour for 1 minute or just until not sticky. Place the dough in an oiled mixing bowl, turning once to coat the ball with oil. Cover and let rise until puffed and doubled in size, about 30 minutes.

2 **Make the sauce:** In a medium saucepan over medium heat, heat the olive oil. Add the onion; cook and stir for 2 to 3 minutes or until softened. Add the garlic; cook and stir for 30 seconds. Add the tomatoes and the juice from the can. Stir in Italian seasoning, sugar, and a pinch each of salt and pepper. Bring the mixture to a boil over high heat. Decrease the heat and simmer, stirring occasionally, until thickened, about 15 minutes.

3 **Make the pizza:** Preheat the oven to 450°F. Oil a 12-inch pizza pan with some olive oil and dust with cornmeal; set aside.

4 Place the pizza dough on a lightly floured surface. Pat and stretch with your hands into a 12-inch circle. Transfer to the prepared pizza pan. Brush lightly with olive oil. Spread about ⅔ cup of the sauce over the dough. (Save the remaining sauce for another use.) Arrange the pepperoni slices and mozzarella evenly over the sauce. Bake until the sauce is bubbly and the crust edges are browned, 8 to 10 minutes.

5 Cut into wedges to serve. Sprinkle with red peppers flakes as desired.

ON-A-HOT-STREAK DOGS

Beginner
Active Time: 45 minutes
Total Time: 45 minutes
Makes 6 servings

A session of sustained success inhaling PAC-DOTS, POWER PELLETS, FRUITS, and GHOSTS can pump up the appetite. Satisfy your hunger with this fiery dog topped with avocado crema, pico de gallo, Cotija cheese, and the secret ingredient—crushed flaming-hot cheese puffs. OH, YEAH!

Unsalted butter, softened

6 hot dog buns

6 all-beef hot dogs or plant-based hot dogs

Avocado Crema (recipe follows)

Pico de Gallo (recipe follows)

3 tablespoons crumbled Cotija cheese

½ cup crushed flaming-hot cheese puffs

FOR GARNISH

Fresh cilantro leaves

1 Preheat a grill to medium-high.

2 Butter the cut sides of the hot dog buns and grill just until golden brown and toasted, 30 seconds to 1 minute (watch carefully so they don't burn!). Set aside.

3 Grill the hot dogs, rotating frequently, until grill marks appear and the hot dogs are lightly charred, 5 to 6 minutes.

4 Place the hot dogs in the buns. Drizzle with the Avocado Crema. Top with the Pico de Gallo, Cotija cheese, and crushed cheese puffs. Garnish with cilantro leaves. Serve immediately.

Avocado Crema: In a mini food processor or blender, combine 1 small ripe avocado, halved, seeded, and coarsely chopped; ⅓ cup Mexican crema or sour cream; 1 tablespoon lime juice; ¼ cup snipped fresh cilantro; and ¼ to ½ teaspoon salt. Blend until smooth. If the mixture is thick, add water, ½ teaspoon at a time, and blend until of drizzling consistency.

Pico de Gallo: In a medium bowl, stir together 2 medium plum tomatoes, chopped; 1 serrano chile, stemmed and finely chopped; 2 tablespoons finely chopped white onion; 2 tablespoons finely chopped cilantro; 1 tablespoon lime juice; and ¼ teaspoon salt.

PAC-MAN MAC & CHEESE

PAC-MAN's round disk shape inspires this creamy homemade mac and cheese made with round, disk-shape orecchiette pasta. A pinch of turmeric bumps up the color of the cheese sauce to resemble PAC-MAN's cheery yellow hue.

FOR BREADCRUMB TOPPING

1 cup fresh breadcrumbs

2 tablespoons unsalted butter, melted

2 tablespoons grated Parmesan cheese

Pinch of cayenne pepper or paprika

8 ounces dried orecchiette pasta

1 teaspoon salt

FOR THE CHEESE SAUCE

3 tablespoons unsalted butter

¼ cup finely chopped onion

2 tablespoons all-purpose flour

2 cups whole milk

Few dashes bottled hot sauce

¾ teaspoon salt

½ teaspoon dry mustard (optional)

Pinch of ground turmeric

4 ounces shredded sharp cheddar or Monterey Jack cheese

8 ounces shredded American cheese

FOR GARNISH

3 or 4 slices ripe tomato

1 Preheat the oven to 350°F. Butter a 1½-quart shallow baking dish; set aside.

2 Make the breadcrumb topping: In a small bowl, stir together the breadcrumbs, melted butter, Parmesan cheese, and cayenne; set aside.

3 In a large saucepan, bring 2 quarts of water to a boil over high heat. Add the pasta and salt; cook and stir until just tender, 6 to 8 minutes. Drain the pasta and rinse with cold water to prevent sticking; set aside.

4 Make the cheese sauce: In the same saucepan, melt the butter. Add the onion and cook, stirring, until tender and translucent, about 2 minutes. Add the flour and whisk to combine. Gradually stir in the milk, whisking constantly to combine. Stir in the hot sauce, salt, dry mustard, if using, and turmeric. Cook and stir over medium-high heat until the mixture comes to a gentle boil. Remove the pan from the heat.

5 Gradually stir in the shredded cheeses. Whisk until smooth. Fold in the cooked pasta until well combined. Transfer to the prepared baking dish. Sprinkle the breadcrumb mixture evenly over the top. Bake until the breadcrumbs are golden brown and the edges of the pasta are bubbly, 20 to 25 minutes. Let stand for 5 to 10 minutes before serving.

6 Cut a wedge out of each of the tomato slices. Garnish the top with the PAC-MAN tomato slices.

BIG-BATCH MAC: You can easily double this recipe to fill a 13-by-9-inch casserole dish.

SMASHING-IT SMASH BURGERS

Beginner
Active Time: 45 minutes
Total Time: 45 minutes
Makes 2 servings

Cleared a level with all of your lives intact? Made a genius move and evaded the treachery of the GHOST GANG? Ate a POWER PELLET and gobbled up a GHOST or four? Hit your high score? Got a Bonus Life? You are SMASHING IT! Keep the theme going with these juicy burgers embellished with crispy, lacy edges and golden brown onions pressed into the patties. They can be cooked on the stovetop in a cast-iron pan or on a grill.

Unsalted butter, softened

2 potato hamburger buns

Burger Sauce (recipe follows)

6 ounces ground beef
(preferably 85% lean)

Salt and black pepper

1 small yellow onion,
very thinly sliced*

2 slices American cheese

2 slices ripe tomato

8 dill pickle chips

2 leaves iceberg or
green leaf lettuce

1 Butter the cut sides of the hamburger buns with softened butter. Heat a large cast-iron skillet over medium-high heat. Toast the buns just until golden brown, 30 seconds to 1 minute (watch carefully so they don't burn!). Spread the Burger Sauce on all cut sides of the buns. Set aside.

2 Divide the ground beef into two 3-ounce portions. Using wet hands, shape each into a patty about 3 inches wide. Season lightly with salt and pepper.

3 Heat the cast-iron skillet over high heat until it's ripping hot. Place the patties in the skillet. Divide the sliced onion between the 2 patties. (They should be piled up pretty high.) Use a burger press or wide, flat metal spatula to vigorously press down on the patties, pressing the onions into the meat. Season the onions lightly with salt and pepper. Cook until the patties are brown and crusty around the edges, 1 to 2 minutes.

4 Using the spatula, loosen the browned, crusty edges all around each patty and carefully flip it onion-side down. Top each patty with a cheese slice and cook until the onions are browned along the edges, 1 to 2 minutes longer.

5 Place the patties cheese-side up on the bun bottoms. Top with tomato, pickles, lettuce, and the bun tops. Serve immediately.

Burger Sauce: In a small bowl, stir together 3 tablespoons mayonnaise, 1 tablespoon ketchup, 1 tablespoon yellow mustard, 2 teaspoons sweet pickle relish, ½ teaspoon sugar, and ½ teaspoon distilled white vinegar. Cover and refrigerate until READY to use.

*Tip: Slice the onions as thinly as you possibly can. If you have a mandoline, use it to slice the onions 1/16 inch thick.

LEVEL 256
PARTY SUB

Beginner
Active Time: 20 minutes
Total Time: 20 minutes
Makes 4 servings

You may still be working on reaching Level 256—the last level of PAC-MAN, also called the "split-screen level" because the right side of the screen turns into a scramble of letters and numbers and the left side looks normal—but you can enjoy this top-level party sub packed with meats, cheeses, and a savory salad anytime.

FOR THE SALAD

2 cups lightly packed chopped romaine lettuce

½ cup lightly packed torn fresh basil

½ cup halved pitted green olives

½ cup halved mild or hot cherry peppers

⅓ cup olive oil

¼ cup white or red wine vinegar

1 teaspoon Dijon mustard

1 teaspoon honey

1 teaspoon dried Italian seasoning blend

1 clove garlic, minced

¼ teaspoon salt

¼ teaspoon black pepper

FOR THE SANDWICH

One 14-inch loaf Italian bread, split lengthwise

8 ounces thinly sliced turkey

8 ounces thinly sliced capicola or ham

6 ounces sliced Genoa salami

4 ounces sliced mozzarella cheese

4 ounces sliced aged provolone cheese

1 **Make the salad:** In a medium bowl, toss together the lettuce, basil, olives, and cherry peppers. In a screw-top jar, combine the oil, vinegar, mustard, honey, seasoning blend, garlic, salt, and black pepper. Cover and shake well. Pour some of the dressing over the salad to lightly coat; toss to combine. Reserve any leftover dressing for another use.

2 **Make the sandwich:** Layer the bottom half of the bread with the turkey, capicola, salami, mozzarella, and provolone. Top with the salad. Hollow out some of the bread from the top of loaf. Add the top of the bread; lightly press. Secure the sub with small skewers and cut into 4 sandwiches.

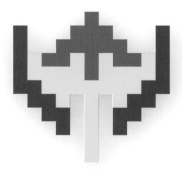

WAKA WAKA WAFFLES

Beginner
Active Time: 20 minutes
Total Time: 35 minutes
Makes 4 servings

WAKA WAKA! It's the beautiful sound of evading GHOSTS, racking up points, and chomping on tasty PAC-DOTS! These whimsical waffle stacks filled with ham and cheese—and topped with a fried egg—are perfect for a quick, light meal or a hearty snack.

Special equipment: Mini waffle maker that makes 4-inch round waffles

FOR THE WAFFLES

1½ cups all-purpose flour

½ cup fine cornmeal

1 teaspoon baking powder

1 teaspoon baking soda

1 teaspoon salt

2 tablespoons sugar

2 cups buttermilk

2 large eggs

¼ cup unsalted butter, melted, divided

4 scallions, finely chopped, plus more for serving

Nonstick cooking spray

FOR THE STACK

4 tablespoons unsalted butter

4 large eggs, divided

Salt and black pepper

4 slices thinly sliced ham

4 slices sharp cheddar cheese

Hot sauce, for serving

1 Place a wire rack on the center rack of the oven. Preheat the oven to 200°F.

2 **Make the waffles:** In a large bowl, stir together the flour, cornmeal, baking powder, baking soda, salt, and sugar.

3 In a medium bowl, whisk together the buttermilk, eggs, and melted butter. Pour into the flour mixture; stir just until combined. Fold in the scallions.

4 Preheat a mini waffle maker to medium heat according to the manufacturer's directions. Coat the iron with cooking spray. Pour the batter onto the iron and cook according to the manufacturer's directions. Gently remove the waffles and transfer to the wire rack to keep warm. Cook the remaining batter. (You should have 8 waffles. Waffles should be golden and tender, and will crisp as they rest.)

5 **Make the stack:** In a well-seasoned large skillet over medium heat, heat 2 tablespoons of the butter until shimmering. Crack 2 of the eggs, one at a time, into a ramekin or small bowl. Carefully slide each egg into the skillet; lightly sprinkle with salt and black pepper. Cook, uncovered, for 1 minute. Cover and cook until the whites are just set and the edges are crisp and golden, about 2 minutes for runny yolks or 2½ minutes for jammy yolks. Transfer to a plate to keep warm. Repeat with the remaining 2 tablespoons butter and remaining 2 eggs.

6 For each stack, place one waffle on a plate; top with a slice of ham, a slice of cheese, and another waffle. Top with a fried egg. Sprinkle with additional scallions, if desired. Serve with hot sauce.

CLYDE'S SHY-GUY POKE BOWLS

Pro
DF
Active Time: 30 minutes
Total Time: 30 minutes
Makes 4 servings

CLYDE—nicknamed POKEY because sometimes he hangs back and moves a little more slowly—is often poking around doing other things while the chase is on. Maybe he's off preparing these poke bowls, which require a fair bit of chopping.

FOR THE POKE

¼ cup soy sauce

2 scallions, chopped

1 tablespoon sesame oil

1 tablespoon rice vinegar

2 teaspoons finely grated ginger

2 teaspoons toasted
sesame seeds

1 teaspoon red pepper flakes

12 ounces sushi-grade
tuna steaks, cubed

**FOR THE WASABI MAYONNAISE
(OPTIONAL)**

½ cup mayonnaise

2 teaspoons wasabi paste

1 teaspoon rice vinegar

½ teaspoon honey

¼ teaspoon sesame oil

FOR THE BOWL

4 cups cooked sushi rice

½ English cucumber, cut
into ½-inch pieces

1 ripe avocado, peeled, seeded,
cut into 8 wedges, and diced

½ cup cooked shelled edamame

½ cup coarsely shredded carrots

2 radishes, sliced

1 **Make the poke:** In a medium bowl, stir together the soy sauce, scallions, sesame oil, vinegar, ginger, sesame seeds, and red pepper flakes. Add the tuna; toss to combine.

2 **Make the wasabi mayonnaise:** In a small bowl, whisk together the mayonnaise, wasabi, vinegar, honey, and sesame oil.

3 **Make the bowl:** Divide the rice among four shallow bowls. Top with the tuna poke, cucumber, avocado, edamame, carrots, and radishes. Drizzle with the Wasabi Mayonnaise, if using.

HOT-PURSUIT HOT POT

Pro
GF, DF
Active Time: 15 minutes
Total Time: 35 minutes
Makes 4 servings

In PAC-MAN, there's a whole lotta chasing going on. In real life, if you're just on the hunt for a fun dinner, a Japanese-style hot pot is the way to go. Proteins and vegetables are cooked in a pot of flavorful broth bubbling away in the center of the table. It encourages lively conversation—maybe even sharing tips for improving your game.

FOR THE PROTEINS AND VEGETABLES

6 ounces chicken breast, very thinly sliced

8 shrimp, peeled and deveined

One 14-ounce block firm tofu, drained, rinsed, and cut into 1-inch cubes

½ head napa cabbage, thinly sliced

4 ounces shiitake mushrooms, trimmed and caps sliced

1 bunch enoki mushrooms, trimmed and cut into 2-inch pieces

1 large carrot, shaved into ribbons

FOR THE BROTH

4 cups dashi (Japanese stock)

¼ cup sake

¼ cup mirin

¼ cup soy sauce

1 teaspoon salt

2 scallions, cut on the diagonal

Shichimi togarashi

1 In the center of the table, set up an electric hot pot or portable stove for a large Dutch oven.

2 **Make the proteins and vegetables:** Arrange the chicken, shrimp, and tofu on a platter. Arrange the cabbage, mushrooms, and carrot on another platter. Place the platters on the table.

3 **Make the broth:** In the pot, combine the dashi, sake, mirin, soy sauce, and salt. Cover; bring to a boil over medium-high heat. In batches, add the ingredients to the pot, arranging them in sections, until the pot is filled (don't overcrowd the pot). Decrease the heat. Simmer, covered, just until done, 6 to 8 minutes.

4 Use a large spoon and chopsticks to serve the cooked food in shallow bowls. Sprinkle with the scallions and togarashi. Bring the broth to a boil and repeat until all of the ingredients have been cooked.

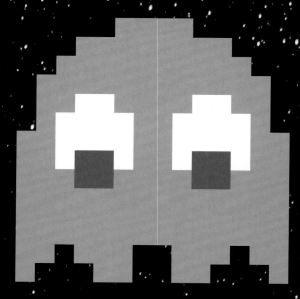

HIGH-SCORING SIDES

Side dishes
are often seen
as minor characters in
the context of a meal, but
PAC-MAN doesn't have any
minor characters. Everyone—from the
ravenous yellow orb himself gorging
on PAC-DOTS to all four of the GHOSTS
menacing him—plays a major role in
creating an exciting, exhilarating game.
These sides—salads, slaws,
veggies, breads, and more—
do the same thing
for dinner.

PAC-MAN CHEESE CORN

Beginner
V, GF
Active Time: 25 minutes
Total Time: 25 minutes
Makes 4 to 6 servings

Blazing through your game with fingers and reflexes aflame? This take on Korean corn cheese is on fire, too—with heat from fresh jalapeño or serrano chile—and a hit of seriously hot (but optional) GHOST pepper powder.

4 cups frozen corn kernels, thawed and drained

¼ cup finely chopped red BELL pepper

1 jalapeño or serrano pepper, finely chopped (seeded if desired)

⅓ cup mayonnaise

1 teaspoon sugar

½ teaspoon salt

¼ teaspoon black pepper

2 tablespoons unsalted butter

1½ cups shredded mozzarella cheese

1 scallion, thinly sliced on the diagonal

GHOST pepper powder (optional)

1 Place an oven rack in the highest position. Preheat the broiler.

2 In a large bowl, combine the corn, BELL pepper, jalapeño, mayonnaise, sugar, salt, and black pepper.

3 In an 8- to 10-inch cast-iron skillet or ovenproof skillet over high heat, melt the butter. Add the corn mixture and cook, stirring frequently, just until warmed, 3 to 4 minutes. Spread the mixture into an even layer, then cover with the mozzarella.

4 Broil until the cheese is melty and golden brown in spots, 3 to 4 minutes (watch carefully so it doesn't burn!).

5 Sprinkle with the scallion and serve. If desired, sprinkle servings with GHOST pepper powder.

FIVE-FRUITS SALAD

Beginner
V, GF, DF
Active Time: 20 minutes
Total Time: 20 minutes
Makes 4 servings

Eat the first five FRUITS in PAC-MAN and rack up 2,600 points! Make this salad featuring CHERRIES (100 points), STRAWBERRIES (300 points), ORANGES (500 points), APPLES (700 points), and MELONS (1,000 points) for a bring-a-dish brunch and you'll win the game, hands down.

FOR THE HONEY VINAIGRETTE

¼ cup honey

¼ cup ORANGE juice

2 teaspoons finely grated lemon zest

2 teaspoons finely chopped fresh mint

FOR THE SALAD

1 cup halved and pitted sweet CHERRIES

2 cups sliced STRAWBERRIES

1 ORANGE, segmented*

1 APPLE, cored and diced

1 cup cubed honeydew MELON

1 **Make the honey vinaigrette:** In a small bowl, whisk together the honey, ORANGE juice, lemon zest, and mint.

2 **Make the salad:** In a medium bowl, combine the CHERRIES, STRAWBERRIES, ORANGE segments, APPLE, and MELON. Drizzle some of the dressing over the FRUIT; toss to coat. Serve immediately.

*__Tip:__ Use a chef's knife to slice a thin piece off both the top and the bottom of the ORANGE so that the flesh is exposed. Place one cut end on the surface of the cutting board. From top to bottom, follow the contour of the FRUIT to cut the peel and white pith away. Holding the peeled FRUIT over a small bowl to catch any juices, use a paring knife to slice along both sides of each membrane inside the ORANGE to loosen and free the individual sections of FRUIT.

BEET THE HIGH SCORE

Beginner
V, GF
Active Time: 15 minutes
Total Time: 55 minutes
Makes 4 servings

Score big points with these colorful roasted beets dressed with a honey-balsamic vinaigrette and topped with ORANGE zest and goat cheese. It's great paired with grilled chicken, pork chops, or pork tenderloin.

6 medium red, gold, and striped (Chioggia) beets, trimmed, peeled, and cut into 1-inch cubes

2 to 3 tablespoons olive oil

1 teaspoon salt

1 teaspoon coarse black pepper

2 tablespoons balsamic vinegar

1 tablespoon honey

1 tablespoon coarsely grated ORANGE zest

¼ cup goat cheese or feta cheese

1 Preheat the oven to 400°F. Line a large rimmed baking sheet with parchment paper.

2 Place the beets on the prepared baking sheet; drizzle with the oil and toss to coat. Sprinkle with the salt and black pepper. Roast until tender when tested with a fork, 40 to 45 minutes.

3 In a small bowl, whisk together the vinegar and honey. Drizzle over the beets and toss to coat. Sprinkle with the ORANGE zest and cheese.

AWESOME SLAW

Beginner
V, GF, DF
Active Time: 15 minutes
Total Time: 45 minutes
Makes 4 to 6 servings

Pull a stellar move and make this light and crunchy vinaigrette-dressed slaw, perfect for serving with burgers, bratwurst, or chicken. To maximize speed, you can substitute 6 cups of prepared tricolor coleslaw mix for the red cabbage, green cabbage, and carrots.

FOR THE VINAIGRETTE

3 tablespoons olive oil

3 tablespoons apple cider vinegar

1 teaspoon finely chopped onion or 1 clove garlic, minced

½ teaspoon Dijon mustard

½ teaspoon honey

½ teaspoon salt

¼ teaspoon coarsely ground black pepper

FOR THE SLAW

½ medium head red cabbage, shredded (3 cups)

¼ medium head green cabbage, shredded (2 cups)

3 medium carrots, coarsely grated (1 cup)

1 cup lightly packed chopped fresh parsley

½ cup lightly packed chopped fresh dill (optional)

2 scallions, green part only, chopped

¼ cup roasted and salted sunflower seeds or sliced almonds

1 **Make the vinaigrette:** In a jar with a tight-fitting lid, combine all of the vinaigrette ingredients. Shake vigorously to thoroughly combine.

2 **Make the slaw:** In a large bowl, combine the cabbage, carrots, parsley, dill, if using, and scallions. Drizzle with the vinaigrette; toss to coat. Cover and chill for at least 30 minutes. Just before serving, sprinkle with the sunflower seeds; toss to combine.

PAC-MAN'S PULL-AWAY CHEESE BREAD

Mid-Level
V
Active Time: 25 minutes
Total Time: 1 hour 40 minutes
Makes 8 servings

Outrun the competition the way PAC-MAN gets ahead of the GHOSTS with this cheesy pesto and sun-dried-tomato pull-apart loaf that's perfect with a big bowl of soup or as a party snack.

One 1-pound loaf frozen bread dough

⅔ cup prepared basil pesto

1 cup shredded mozzarella cheese

⅓ cup finely chopped sun-dried tomatoes, chopped olives, or pine nuts

2 tablespoons grated Parmesan cheese

1 Thaw the bread dough according to the package directions. If thawed in the refrigerator, let stand at room temperature for 30 minutes. Grease a 9-by-4-inch loaf pan. Line the pan with strips of parchment paper; set aside.

2 Place the dough on a lightly floured work surface and cut into 1-inch pieces. Place the pesto in a small bowl. Dip about one-quarter of the dough pieces in the pesto and arrange them in the bottom of the prepared loaf pan. Sprinkle one-third of the mozzarella and one-third of the sun-dried tomatoes over the dough pieces. Repeat dipping and layering the dough, mozzarella, and sun-dried tomatoes two more times. Dip remaining quarter of dough balls in remaining quarter of the pesto and arrange on top. (You will have four layers of dough balls and three layers of cheese and tomatoes.) Sprinkle the Parmesan cheese on top. Cover and let rise in a warm place until nearly double in size, about 45 minutes.

3 Preheat the oven to 350°F.

4 Bake the loaf until golden brown and done in the center, 30 to 40 minutes. Cover with foil during the last 10 minutes to prevent overbrowning.

5 Use the parchment paper strips to lift the loaf from the pan while still hot. Let cool slightly on a wire rack. Peel away the parchment paper and serve warm. Pull apart to serve.

BLINKY'S TENACIOUS TOMATO SOUP

Beginner
V
Active Time: 30 minutes
Total Time: 45 minutes
Makes 6 to 8 servings

Red pepper flakes bring the fire to this bold tomato soup like BLINKY brings the heat as the leader of the GHOST GANG. Be like BLINKY—dogged, dedicated, determined, and hard to shake!

3 tablespoons unsalted butter

½ cup chopped onion

2 tablespoons all-purpose flour

2 tablespoons tomato paste

2 teaspoons salt

1 teaspoon brown sugar

½ teaspoon baking soda

¼ to ½ teaspoon red pepper flakes, plus more as needed

Two 14-ounce cans fire-roasted diced tomatoes, undrained

One 28-ounce can crushed tomatoes

¾ cup chicken or vegetable broth

1 bay leaf

½ cup heavy cream

4 slices French bread, toasted

6 to 8 pitted black olives, halved

Freshly ground black pepper

1 In a large pot over medium heat, melt the butter. Add the onion and cook, stirring, until the pieces are translucent, about 3 minutes. Add the flour and stir briskly until combined. Stir in the tomato paste, salt, brown sugar, baking soda, and red pepper flakes. Cook, stirring, for 30 seconds. Stir in the diced tomatoes and their juice, crushed tomatoes, chicken broth, and bay leaf. Increase the heat and bring to a simmer. Simmer, uncovered, for 15 minutes.

2 Remove from the heat; discard the bay leaf. Use an immersion blender to blend until smooth. (Or blend the soup in batches in a regular blender.) Stir in the heavy cream.

3 For an eyeball garnish, use a small, 1-inch cookie cutter to cut round croutons from the toast slices. Place an olive half on each crouton. To serve, ladle the soup into bowls. Arrange two eyeball croutons on top of each soup. Top with additional red pepper flakes or freshly ground black pepper, if desired.

MISSING WEDGE SALAD

Beginner
GF
Active Time: 30 minutes
Total Time: 30 minutes
Makes 4 servings

PAC-MAN is known for his ever-munching mouth. His bottomless hunger just might be satisfied by this CLASSIC wedge salad: crunchy iceberg lettuce, tomatoes, red onion, bacon, and buttermilk–blue cheese dressing.

FOR THE BLUE CHEESE DRESSING

⅔ cup mayonnaise

2 teaspoons apple cider vinegar

3 tablespoons buttermilk

½ teaspoon sugar

¼ cup crumbled blue cheese

Salt and black pepper

FOR THE SALAD

4 slices bacon

3 tablespoons water

1 tablespoon balsamic vinegar

¼ small red onion, thinly sliced

1 cup grape tomatoes,
halved or quartered

1 small head iceberg lettuce,
trimmed and quartered

Blue cheese crumbles (optional)

1 **Make the blue cheese dressing:** In a small bowl, combine the mayonnaise, cider vinegar, buttermilk, and sugar. Stir in the blue cheese and salt and pepper to taste; set aside. (Can be made ahead and refrigerated.)

2 **Make the salad:** In a large skillet over medium heat, cook the bacon until crisp and brown, 6 to 8 minutes. Transfer to a paper towel–lined plate to drain. Pour off the excess bacon grease. Add the water to the hot skillet to deglaze, stirring to loosen any browned bits from the bottom. Remove the skillet from the heat. Add the balsamic vinegar, red onion, and tomatoes. Stir and let stand for 5 minutes.

3 To serve, place the lettuce wedges on salad plates. Spoon the blue cheese dressing over each wedge. Spoon the tomato mixture and juices over the top. Crumble the bacon and sprinkle over the salads along with additional blue cheese, if desired. Sprinkle the salads with additional salt and pepper, as desired.

GHOST WAFFLE CHIPS WITH CURRY KETCHUP

While waffling will only get you in trouble as you speed through the MAZE, making these homemade waffle fries is always a good idea. Serve with a slightly spicy curry ketchup to keep things hopping.

FOR THE FRIES

2 pounds large russet potatoes, peeled

1 teaspoon dried parsley flakes, crushed

1 teaspoon kosher salt

½ teaspoon black pepper

½ teaspoon onion powder

¼ teaspoon garlic powder

2 quarts peanut or canola oil, for frying

FOR THE CURRY KETCHUP

1 tablespoon unsalted butter

¼ cup minced yellow onion

1½ teaspoons curry powder

½ teaspoon smoked paprika

Pinch of cayenne pepper

1 cup ketchup

½ cup water

1 **Make the fries:** Fill a large bowl with ice water. Use a waffle fry cutter or a mandoline fitted with a waffle blade to cut the potatoes into ¼-inch slices. First cut crosswise, then rotate the potato 90 degrees between each cut. Use a large chef's knife to cut each oval slice in half across the shorter length of the potato slice to create two GHOST shapes. Chill for 30 minutes.

2 In a small bowl, stir together the parsley flakes, salt, pepper, onion powder, and garlic powder. Set aside.

3 **Make the curry ketchup:** In a small saucepan over medium heat, melt the butter. Add the onion and cook until soft, about 3 minutes. Add the curry powder, smoked paprika, and cayenne and cook until the spices are toasted, about 1 minute. Add the ketchup and water. Simmer until thick, about 25 minutes. Set aside.

4 Line a large rimmed baking pan with paper towels. Heat the peanut oil in a large Dutch oven over medium heat until it reaches 260°F. Add a piece of potato to the pot. If the oil is hot enough, it will sink and tiny bubbles will rise up from it.

5 Drain the potato slices and rinse under cold water. Arrange in a single layer on a large clean dish towel (or paper towels); pat the potatoes dry. Working in three or four batches, add the potatoes and fry, stirring with a slotted spoon to prevent sticking, for 3 minutes. Use the slotted spoon to transfer to the prepared baking pan in a single layer. (The potatoes will be slightly softened and will have no color.)

6 Line a second baking pan with paper towels or set a wire rack on top of it. Increase the heat to medium-high and heat the oil to 350°F. Add a piece of potato. If the oil is hot enough, it will rise to the top of the oil and bubble vigorously.

7 Working in two or three batches, fry the waffle fries until golden brown and crispy, 2 to 3 minutes, turning each fry once for even browning. Transfer to the second baking sheet. Sprinkle with the seasoning blend. Serve with the curry ketchup for dipping.

BREAKOUT BEVERAGES

Sip as you zip through the MAZE. Stay focused, hydrated, energized, and refreshed for the battle with these beverages ranging from a spiced hot mocha to an invigorating FRUIT slushie, depending on the season and the vibe. Pair the appropriate beverage with a CHAMPION SNACK or two to really up your gastronomical game.

PAC-DOT BUBBLE TEA

Beginner
V, GF
Active Time: 45 minutes
Total Time: 2 hours 45 minutes
Makes 2 servings

PAC-MAN gets fueled up for more conquest by consuming an endless supply of PAC-DOTS. Dominate your day by taking a break with this vivifying mango bubble tea packed with chewy boba balls that are as satisfying to chomp on as those pleasing, point-boosting POWER PELLETS.

Special equipment: Bubble tea straws or long spoons

FOR THE SIMPLE SYRUP

1 cup sugar

1 cup water

1 teaspoon vanilla extract

One 3-inch cinnamon stick

2 whole cloves

FOR THE BOBA AND TEA

2 quarts water

1 cup dried white quick-cooking boba tapioca pearls

1½ cups boiling water

2 bags peach-flavor black tea

FOR ASSEMBLY AND SERVING

1½ cups mango nectar

2 tablespoons vanilla protein powder

Crushed ice

¼ cup light cream or half-and-half

Bubble tea straws or long spoons

1 **Make the simple syrup:** In a small saucepan, combine the sugar, water, vanilla, cinnamon stick, and cloves. Bring just to a simmer, stirring to dissolve the sugar. Remove from the heat and let stand for 10 minutes. Strain into a small bowl. Chill until cold.

2 **Make the boba and tea:** In a large saucepan, bring the 2 quarts water to a boil over medium-high heat. Add the boba pearls; decrease the heat to a simmer. Cook until the boba float to the top of the water, about 8 minutes. Cover the pan with a lid and remove from the heat. Let stand for 8 minutes. Drain the boba in a strainer; rinse with cold water. Add the boba to the chilled syrup. Chill until completely cool, about 1 hour.

3 Pour the 1½ cups boiling water over the tea bags in a measuring cup. Let steep for 5 minutes. Remove the tea bags; chill the tea until cold, about 1 hour.

4 **Assemble and serve the bubble teas:** Spoon about ½ cup of the boba and syrup into the bottoms of two or three tall drink glasses. In a medium pitcher, combine the peach tea, mango nectar, and protein powder. Place a large scoop of ice in each glass, filling the glasses three-quarters full. Pour the mango mixture over the ice. Pour the light cream on top and add a bubble tea straw. Garnish with a few more boba pearls on top.

INKY DRINK

Beginner
V+, GF, DF
Active Time: 5 minutes
Total Time: 15 minutes
Makes 6 servings

Parched from the chase? Quench your thirst with this fizzy blue beverage made with butterfly pea flower powder and a nose-tingling homemade ginger syrup topped off with a splash of club soda.

6 cups water (filtered, if possible)

2 tablespoons butterfly pea flower powder

2 tablespoons Ginger Syrup (recipe follows)

Ice cubes

Club soda, chilled

1 Add the water to a teakettle. Heat over medium heat until hot but not boiling. Add the butterfly pea flower powder; let stand for 10 minutes. Stir in the syrup. Let cool.

2 Fill six tall glasses with ice cubes; add the drink mixture to about three-fourths full. Top with club soda.

Ginger Syrup: In a small saucepan over medium heat, stir together 1 cup water, 1 cup sugar, and ½ cup peeled and chopped fresh ginger. Cook, stirring occasionally, until the mixture comes to a boil and the sugar is dissolved. Remove from the heat. Let stand for 15 to 30 minutes. Use a fine-mesh sieve to strain into a jar or bottle. Let cool completely. Secure the lid and refrigerate for up to 3 weeks.

FRUIT SLUSHIES

Beginner
V+, GF, DF
Active Time: 30 minutes
Total Time: 1 hour 30 minutes
Makes 6 servings

When your game is on fire—or when your day feels like a MAZE you're racing through, with twists of fortune, unanticipated events, and surprises at every turn—take a break and cool down with these refreshing slushies inspired by the CLASSIC FRUITS.

4 cups frozen cut-up FRUIT of choice (CHERRIES, STRAWBERRIES, ORANGE segments, or honeydew MELON)

1½ cups 100% juice or juice blend*

¼ cup Simple Syrup (recipe follows)

2 to 3 cups ice cubes

FOR GARNISH
Fresh mint leaves (optional)

1 Place a loaf pan in the freezer to chill. In a blender, combine the FRUIT, juice, and Simple Syrup. Blend until smooth. Add the ice; blend until slushy, stopping to scrape the sides of the blender occasionally. Pour the mixture into the cold loaf pan. Freeze for 1 to 2 hours or until mostly frozen, stirring occasionally to break up large pieces of ice and to help the mixture freeze evenly.

2 Stir the frozen mixture to break it up before spooning into glasses to serve. If you like, garnish with mint.

Simple Syrup: In a small saucepan over medium heat, combine 1 cup sugar and 1½ cups water. Cook, stirring, until the sugar dissolves. Cool completely.

***Tip:** Choose a juice that directly matches (i.e., CHERRY juice with CHERRIES, ORANGE juice with ORANGES) or complements your FRUIT of choice.

IN-THE-ZONE CONCENTRATION COFFEE

Beginner
V, GF
Active Time: 5 minutes
Total Time: 10 minutes
Makes 2 servings

Get your best game on with this caffeinated coffee treat sweetened with brown sugar and flavored with ground cinnamon, cocoa powder, chile powder, and nutmeg. It will put you in the zone.

½ cup whole milk or oat milk

2 tablespoons brown sugar

2 tablespoons Dutch-process cocoa powder, plus more for garnish

½ teaspoon ground cinnamon, plus more for garnish

½ teaspoon vanilla extract

¼ teaspoon chile powder

⅛ teaspoon ground nutmeg

1½ cups strong-brewed coffee

½ cup heavy cream

1 tablespoon granulated sugar

1 Place a small bowl and the beaters of an electric mixer in the freezer.

2 In a 2-cup glass measuring cup or a small bowl, whisk together the milk, brown sugar, cocoa powder, cinnamon, vanilla, chile powder, and nutmeg until well combined. Divide between two mugs. Add the hot coffee; whisk until combined.

3 In the chilled small bowl, combine the cream and granulated sugar. Beat with the chilled beaters on medium-high speed until soft peaks form (tips curl). Spoon some of the whipped cream on top of the spiced coffee. Use a fine-mesh sieve to sift cocoa powder and/or cinnamon on top.

PERFECT MATCH MATCHA LATTE

Beginner
V, GF
Active Time: 5 minutes
Total Time: 10 minutes
Makes 1 serving

The pursuit of a perfect match—3,333,360 points without losing a life—is the dream of every PAC-MAN player. While you're at it, get Zen with this creamy latte made with ceremonial-grade matcha. The ultimate goal requires the highest grade of rejuvenation!

1½ teaspoons ceremonial-grade matcha

2 tablespoons hot water (not boiling)

1 teaspoon Vanilla Syrup (recipe follows)

¾ cup whole milk or barista-style oat milk

1 Use a fine-mesh strainer to sift the matcha into a mug. Add the hot water and syrup; briskly whisk in a "W" shape until no lumps remain and it's slightly frothy, about 45 seconds.

2 Use an espresso machine* with a steaming wand to steam the milk. Pour the steamed milk into the center of the matcha, ending with the foam.

Vanilla Syrup: In a small saucepan over medium heat, stir together 1 cup water and 1 cup sugar. Cook, stirring occasionally, until the mixture comes to a boil and the sugar is dissolved. Remove from the heat. Add 1 vanilla bean, split lengthwise. Let stand for 3 hours. Use a fine-mesh sieve to strain into a jar or bottle. Let cool completely. Secure the lid and refrigerate for up to 3 weeks.

***Tip:** Or, in a small saucepan, heat the milk to 145°F. Use a handheld milk frother to froth the milk until foamy, about 15 seconds. Pour the steamed milk into the center of the matcha, ending with the foam.

PINKY'S PINK GRAPEFRUIT AMBUSH

Beginner
V+, GF, DF
Active Time: 15 minutes
Total Time: 15 minutes
Makes 4 servings

This pretty pink drink looks innocent enough, but it's got a zippy surprise inspired by PINKY's preferred method of attack—the ambush—but with a much more pleasant outcome! A splash of Jalapeño Simple Syrup brings some unseen and unsuspected heat to this fresh grapefruit-ade.

1 cup freshly squeezed ruby red or pink grapefruit juice

¼ cup superfine granulated sugar

3 cups cold water

2 tablespoons Jalapeño Simple Syrup (recipe follows), or to taste

Ice cubes

Grapefruit slices and jalapeño slices, for garnish

1 In a large pitcher or glass jar, combine the grapefruit juice and sugar. Stir until the sugar dissolves. Add the water and stir again to incorporate. Stir in the Jalapeño Simple Syrup. Taste and add more syrup, if desired.

2 Fill four glasses with ice. Pour the mixture over the ice. Garnish with grapefruit slices and jalapeño slices.

Jalapeño Simple Syrup: In a small saucepan over medium-high heat, bring 1 cup water to a boil. Add 2 cups sugar. Stir constantly until the sugar dissolves completely. Add 2 sliced jalapeños to the pan. Decrease the heat and simmer for 3 minutes, stirring frequently. Remove from the heat and let the syrup steep for 20 minutes. Strain through a fine-mesh strainer into a jar or bottle and let cool completely. Secure the lid and refrigerate for up to 3 weeks.

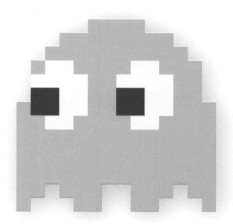

PAC-MAN'S LEMON DROP SIPPER WITH A CHASER

Beginner
V+, GF, DF
Active Time: 30 minutes
Total Time: 30 minutes
Makes 2 servings

It's all about that chase! This unique beverage duo pairs an invigorating lemony mocktail with a fresh, clean chaser that will keep you as cool as a cucumber. Sip one, sip the other, and play on!

FOR THE CUCUMBER-MINT CHASER

½ English cucumber, cut into chunks (no need to peel)

3 tablespoons roughly chopped fresh mint leaves, plus whole leaves for garnish

2 tablespoons fresh lime juice

2 teaspoons Simple Syrup (page 117)

One 1-inch piece fresh ginger, peeled

1 cup cold water

1 tablespoon kosher salt

1 lime wedge

FOR THE LEMON DROP SIPPER

2 tablespoons sugar

1 lemon wedge

Ice cubes

1 cup fresh lemon juice

¼ cup Simple Syrup (page 117)

⅔ cup club soda or sparkling water, chilled

2 lemon twists, for garnish

1 **Make the cucumber-mint chaser:** In a blender, combine the cucumber, mint, lime juice, Simple Syrup, ginger, and water. Blend until smooth.

2 Pour the mixture into a fine-mesh strainer held over a wide-mouth glass jar or a bowl and press with the back of a large spoon to extract as much of the liquid as possible. Discard the pulp. Chill the cucumber-mint juice, covered, in the refrigerator until READY to use.

3 When READY to serve, pour the salt onto a small plate. Moisten the rims of two chilled shot glasses with the lime wedge, if desired. Dip the rims of the glasses in the salt to coat. Divide the chilled cucumber-mint juice between the glasses. Garnish with mint leaves and serve with the Lemon Drop Sipper.

4 **Make the lemon drop sipper:** Pour the sugar onto a small plate. Moisten the rims of two chilled martini glasses with the lemon wedge. Dip the rims of the glasses into the sugar to coat.

5 In a cocktail shaker half-filled with ice, combine the lemon juice and Simple Syrup. Cover and shake vigorously for about 15 seconds. Divide between the two martini glasses. Add the club soda and garnish with a lemon twist. Serve with the Cucumber-Mint Chaser.

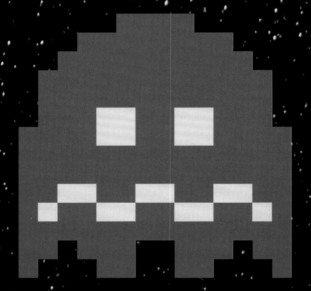

GAME-OVER DESSERTS

When you earn your first
FRUIT, catch up to the
KEY, gain another life, or
hit your all-time high score, celebrate
with something sweet. You earned it!
These cakes, cupcakes, frozen treats,
and more are the perfect way to cap off
a great game or a very good day. (Or to
make you feel a whole lot better
if everything didn't go your
way—this time!)

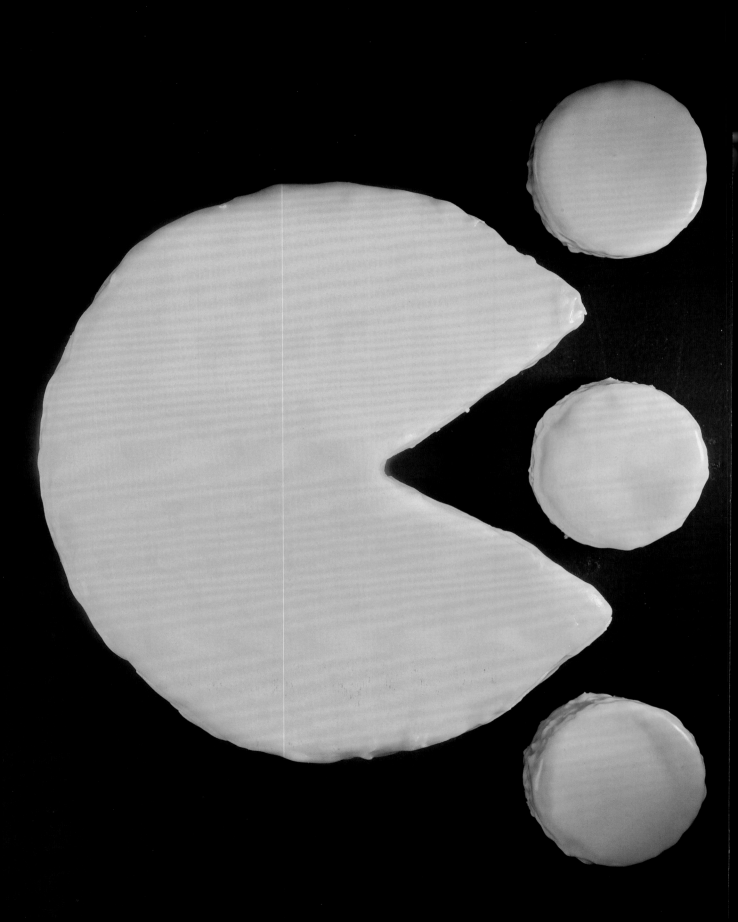

GOBBLE-THEM-UP MINI CAKES

Mid-Level

V

Active Time: 2 hours

Total Time: 3 hours

Makes 10 servings

You'll gobble up these whimsical vanilla butter cakes glazed with white chocolate fondant icing faster than PAC-MAN inhales a line of PAC-DOTS. Arranged on a black serving platter, they pop as brightly as the characters zipping around your screen.

FOR THE CAKE

2½ cups cake flour or all-purpose flour, plus more for dusting pan

2½ teaspoons baking powder

½ teaspoon salt

¾ cup unsalted butter, softened

1¾ cups granulated sugar

3 eggs, at room temperature

1 teaspoon vanilla extract

1¼ cups milk

FOR THE FONDANT ICING

10 ounces quality white baking chocolate, chopped

8 cups sifted powdered sugar

½ cup light corn syrup

½ cup hot water

2 teaspoons vanilla extract

Golden yellow paste food coloring

Peach paste food coloring

1 **Make the cake:** Preheat the oven to 325°F. Grease an 11-by-16-inch or 10-by-15-inch jelly roll pan. Dust the greased pan with flour or line with parchment paper; set aside.

2 In a medium bowl, whisk together the flour, baking powder, and salt; set aside.

3 In a large mixing bowl, beat the butter with an electric mixer on medium-high speed for 30 seconds. Gradually beat in the granulated sugar, adding it ¼ cup at a time, beating until fluffy, about 3 minutes. Add the eggs, one at a time, beating well after each addition. Beat in the vanilla. Alternately add portions of the flour mixture and the milk, beating on low speed until the batter is well combined and smooth. Scrape the sides of the bowl with a rubber spatula as needed. Pour the batter into the prepared pan and smooth the top.

4 Bake until a toothpick inserted into the center of the cake comes out clean, 15 to 20 minutes. Let cool in the pan for 10 minutes. Remove the cake from the pan and place on a wire rack. Freeze the cake for at least 1 hour or until very firm. (The cake will cut better when frozen.) Place the frozen cake on a cutting board for cutting.

5 To prepare cakes for decorating, make a 7-inch PAC-MAN pattern out of cardboard. Cover the pattern with foil. Place the pattern on top of the frozen cake and use a sharp serrated knife to cut out the cake around the pattern. Place the PAC-MAN cake on top of the pattern for support while decorating and serving. Place the cake (and cardboard) on a wire rack. For PAC-DOTS, use a 1½-inch round cookie or biscuit cutter to cut out as many circles as you can from the remaining frozen cake. Place the PAC-DOT cakes on the wire rack. Place a large sheet pan under the rack to catch icing drips; set aside.

6 **Make the fondant icing:** In a small heavy saucepan or in a metal bowl set over simmering water, melt the white chocolate over very low heat. Do not overheat or the chocolate will scorch. Set aside.

7 In another heatproof bowl or the top of a double boiler, combine the powdered sugar, corn syrup, and hot water. Stir with a rubber spatula until the mixture is smooth, scraping the sides and bottom of the bowl. (Do not whisk as you do not want to create bubbles in the icing.) Stir in the melted chocolate until very smooth. Stir in the vanilla.

Recipe continues on next page . . .

8 Place the bowl over a pan of simmering water. Heat and stir gently until the fondant is a nice pourable consistency (about 100°F). If the fondant is still too thick at this temperature, stir in a tiny amount of water until the desired consistency is reached. It should pour off your spatula in a thin stream but still be thick enough to coat the cakes. Keep the icing warm over barely simmering water.

9 To coat the PAC-MAN cake, remove about one-third of the icing from the bowl and stir in enough food coloring to make the icing PAC-MAN yellow. Carefully spoon enough fondant icing over the cake to cover the top and sides. Tint the remaining fondant icing in the bowl a very pale peach color. Place a PAC-DOT on top of a fork over the pale peach fondant and spoon enough icing over to cover the top and sides. Return the cake to the wire rack to set up. Coat all of the remaining PAC-DOTS with the icing. Let set until the icing is firm.

10 Transfer the PAC-MAN cake (on its cardboard base) to one end of a large black serving platter. Use a small metal spatula to transfer the PAC-DOTS to the platter in front of the PAC-MAN cake.

Note: Don't skip creating the cardboard base—it will help prevent the fondant icing from cracking when the cake is transferred to the platter. The cardboard gets covered by icing and won't show. Also, there will likely be leftover icing, but you want to be sure to have enough for adequate coverage of the cakes.

PINKY'S GHOST MOCHI

Mid-Level
V, GF
Active Time: 45 minutes
Total Time: 2 hours 45 minutes
Makes 6 to 8 mochi

Mochi are soft and squishy inside. Given her reputation as a strategic schemer, PINKY is anything but. She is speedy, though, and when you're craving something sweet—like, now—it's a great strategy to have a batch of these ice cream treats in the freezer.

1 pint STRAWBERRY or vanilla ice cream

1 cup glutinous rice flour (also called sweet rice flour)

¼ cup granulated sugar

2 tablespoons powdered sugar

2 tablespoons cornstarch, plus more for dusting

1 cup water

Pink food coloring

1 To freeze ice cream balls, use a small ice cream scoop to form six to eight 1½-inch ice cream balls and place on a parchment paper towel–lined tray. Freeze for at least 1 hour or until very firm.

2 To make mochi, in a medium microwave-safe bowl, combine the rice flour, granulated sugar, powdered sugar, and cornstarch. Add the water and food coloring; stir well until smooth. Cover the bowl with plastic wrap; microwave for 1 minute. Fold and stir the dough with a rubber spatula. Cover and microwave again for 1 minute. Fold and stir the dough again. Microwave in 30-second increments until the dough is shiny and thick.

3 Line a work surface with parchment paper. Dust the paper well with additional cornstarch. Turn the hot dough out onto the cornstarch and let stand until cool enough to handle. Sprinkle the top of the dough ball with additional cornstarch. Use a rolling pin to roll the dough to ¼ inch thick. Transfer the parchment paper with the dough to a baking sheet or tray and place in the refrigerator for 30 minutes.

4 Remove the dough from the refrigerator. Use a 4-inch round cookie or biscuit cutter to cut out 6 to 8 rounds from the dough. Make one mochi ball at a time by brushing the excess cornstarch from a dough circle. Place a frozen ice cream ball in the center of the dough (leave the remaining ice cream balls in the freezer). Gently wrap the dough circle around the ice cream; pinch the edges of the dough to seal and place on the tray in the freezer, seam-side down. Repeat with the remaining dough and ice cream. Freeze for 1 hour. Serve the same day or store in a tightly sealed container in the freezer for up to 3 months.

Green Tea Ice Cream Variation: Stir 1 teaspoon matcha powder into the softened vanilla ice cream. Freeze the mixture until firm before scooping into balls. Tint the mochi dough a light green color.

Tip: If the balls get too soft as you are forming them, you can wrap them individually in plastic wrap immediately after shaping to help hold their shape. Twist the plastic wrap tightly at the bottom of the mochi ball and place in the freezer immediately.

133

PAC-MAN LEMON-CHERRY CHEESECAKE

Pro
V
Active Time: 45 minutes
Total Time: 1 hour 45 minutes
+ chilling
Makes 10 servings

PAC-MAN's interminably munching mouth is about a 90-degree angle at its maximum—one-quarter of his entire body. This ethereal Japanese-style cheesecake is so light and fluffy, you may be tempted to eat one-quarter of it in a single sitting.

5 large eggs, divided

¼ teaspoon cream of tartar

½ cup sugar, divided

One 8-ounce package cream cheese, softened

¼ cup unsalted butter, softened

½ cup milk

1 tablespoon lemon juice

¼ cup all-purpose flour

2 tablespoons cornstarch

1 tablespoon lemon zest

CHERRY Sauce (recipe follows)

1 Separate the egg yolks from the egg whites. Place the whites in a large mixing bowl and place the yolks in a small bowl. Let stand at room temperature for 30 minutes.

2 Preheat the oven to 325°F. Fill a 9-by-13-inch baking pan with 1 inch of hot water and place in the oven on the lowest rack. Lightly grease an 8-inch springform pan. Wrap the outside of the pan with foil to prevent leaking in the hot water bath. Line the bottom of the pan with a circle of parchment paper. Cut a 5-inch-wide strip of parchment paper and use to line the inner sides of the pan; set aside.

3 Add the cream of tartar to the egg whites; beat with an electric mixer on medium speed until foamy. Gradually add ¼ cup of the sugar. Beat on high speed, scraping the sides of the bowl occasionally, until soft peaks form. Set aside.

4 In another bowl, beat the cream cheese until soft and creamy. Beat in the butter and egg yolks until well combined. Gradually beat in the milk and lemon juice until smooth.

5 In a small bowl, whisk together the remaining ¼ cup sugar, flour, and cornstarch. Add to the cream cheese mixture and beat on low speed just until combined. Stir in the lemon zest.

6 Gently fold one-third of the beaten egg whites into the cream cheese mixture. Fold in the remaining egg whites until combined and no white streaks remain, being careful not to break up the egg whites too much. Pour into the prepared pan. Place the pan in the hot water bath in the oven. Bake until a toothpick inserted into the center comes out clean, 60 to 70 minutes.

7 Turn off oven and open oven door slightly. Let cake cool in oven for 1 hour. Remove pan from water bath and remove the foil. Loosen the sides of springform pan and refrigerate for several hours or until well chilled. Cut into wedges and serve with CHERRY Sauce.

CHERRY Sauce: In a medium saucepan over medium heat, combine ½ cup sugar, 2 tablespoons cornstarch, and ½ cup cold water. Add 2 cups fresh or frozen (and thawed) pitted tart CHERRIES. Cook and stir until thickened and bubbly. Cook and stir 2 minutes longer. Remove from the heat. Stir in ½ teaspoon almond extract. Transfer to a bowl; cover and chill for at least 1 hour.

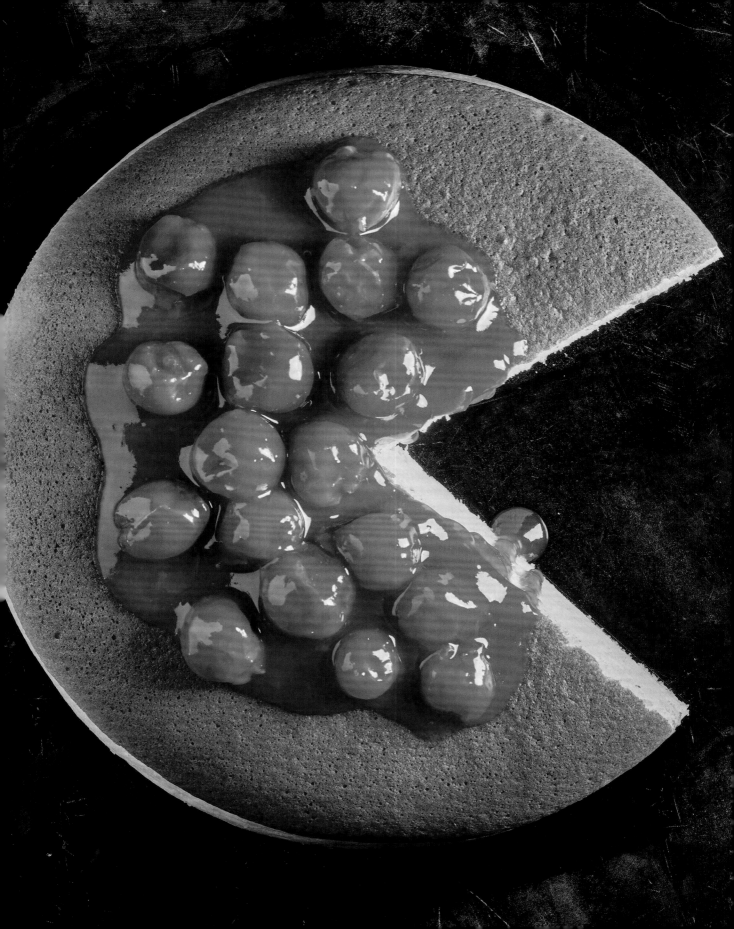

PEANUT BUTTER–OATMEAL GHOST COOKIES

Beginner
V
Active Time: 30 minutes
Total Time: 50 minutes
Makes about 3 dozen cookies

However you see your apparitional attackers—as GHOSTS, MONSTERS, or even GHOST MONSTERS—you'll see nothing but tastiness in these chunky treats inspired by CLASSIC MONSTER cookies. In this version, BLINKY, PINKY, INKY, and CLYDE each get their very own customized cookie.

½ cup unsalted butter, softened

½ cup creamy peanut butter

1 cup brown sugar

½ cup granulated sugar

1 teaspoon baking soda

1 teaspoon ground cinnamon

1 teaspoon salt

2 large eggs

1 teaspoon vanilla extract

1½ cups all-purpose flour

3 cups regular or quick-cooking rolled oats

1 cup white chocolate or semisweet chocolate chips

½ cup sweetened flaked coconut (optional)

½ cup each color of candy-coated chocolate candies (GHOST colors of red, blue, pink, and orange)

3 tablespoons each color of oblong sprinkles (red, blue, pink, and orange)

1 Preheat the oven to 350°F. Line two large rimmed baking sheets with parchment paper.

2 In a large mixing bowl, beat the butter and peanut butter with an electric mixer on medium speed for 30 seconds to combine. Add the brown sugar, granulated sugar, baking soda, cinnamon, and salt; beat on medium-high speed for 2 minutes or until fluffy. Beat in the eggs and vanilla until well combined. Beat in the flour on low speed. Stir in the oats, chocolate chips, and coconut, if using. Divide the dough equally into four bowls. Stir one color of candy and sprinkles into each of the bowls.

3 Drop dough by rounded tablespoons onto the prepared baking sheets. Bake the cookies, one sheet at a time, until lightly browned, 10 to 12 minutes. Let cool on the sheet for a few minutes; remove with a spatula to a wire rack to cool completely.

PAC-MAN DESSERT PIZZA

Mid-Level

V

Active Time: 45 minutes
Total Time: 1 hour 45 minutes
Makes 12 servings

PAC-MAN looks like a pizza with a slice cut out—and it doesn't always have to be sausage or pepperoni. This PAC-MAN-inspired dessert pizza has a sugar-cookie crust topped with an ORANGE-infused cream cheese–sour cream spread, fresh FRUIT, and a jelly glaze. Sweet!

FOR THE COOKIE CRUST

1 cup unsalted butter, softened

1 cup sugar

½ teaspoon salt

2 egg yolks

1 teaspoon vanilla extract

1 teaspoon ORANGE extract (optional)

1 cup yellow cornmeal

1½ cups all-purpose flour

2 teaspoons ORANGE zest

FOR THE CREAM CHEESE TOPPING

One 8-ounce package cream cheese, softened

¼ cup sour cream

2 tablespoons sugar

1 teaspoon ORANGE zest

2 teaspoons ORANGE juice

FOR THE FRUIT TOPPING

3 mandarin ORANGES, peeled and separated into sections

1 ripe mango, peeled, pitted, and sliced

1 ripe peach, peeled, pitted, and cut into small pieces

½ ripe pineapple, peeled, cored, and cut into bite-size pieces

Any other golden FRUIT in season (starfruit, golden kiwi, golden raspberries, etc.)

¼ cup APPLE jelly, melted

Yellow and orange edible flowers (optional)

Fresh mint leaves

1 **Make the cookie crust:** Preheat the oven to 350°F. Grease a 12-inch pizza pan; set aside.

2 In a large mixing bowl, beat the butter with an electric mixer on medium speed for 30 seconds. Add the sugar and salt; beat for 2 minutes until fluffy. Beat in the egg yolks, vanilla, and ORANGE extract, if using, until combined. Beat in the cornmeal and as much flour as you can with the mixer. Stir in the remaining flour and ORANGE zest. Spread the dough evenly in the prepared pizza pan. Bake until golden brown on the edges and set in the center, 20 to 25 minutes. Let cool in the pan on a wire rack.

3 **Make the cream cheese topping:** In a medium bowl, combine the cream cheese, sour cream, and sugar. Beat with an electric mixer on medium-high speed until smooth. Stir in the ORANGE zest and juice. Spread the cream cheese mixture over the cooled crust.

4 **Make the FRUIT topping:** Arrange the FRUITS over the cream cheese layer in an attractive pattern. Brush the FRUIT with the APPLE jelly. Cover and chill for up to 2 hours. Garnish with edible flowers, if using, and mint leaves. Cut into wedges to serve.

GHOST CAKE POPS

Mid-Level
V
Active Time: 2 hours
Total Time: 3 hours
Makes 24 cake pops

You don't need to eat a POWER PELLET to render this GHOST GANG edible—enjoy them in just a few sweet bites. Eat all four and you'll win a 1,600-point bonus!

FOR THE MARSHMALLOW FONDANT

One 16-ounce package mini marshmallows

2 tablespoons water

8 cups sifted powdered sugar, divided

¼ cup vegetable shortening

Gel paste food coloring (GHOST colors of red, blue, pink, and orange)

FOR THE FROSTING

½ cup unsalted butter, softened

2½ cups powdered sugar

1 teaspoon vanilla extract

1 tablespoon milk

FOR THE CAKE BALLS

One 15-ounce package white or vanilla cake mix, prepared according to package directions, cooled

Two 10-ounce packages white chocolate melting wafers, divided

24 cake pop sticks

48 small candy eyes

1 **Make the marshmallow fondant:** Place the marshmallows and water in a large microwave-safe bowl. Microwave on high for 1 minute; stir. Microwave in 30-second increments, stirring after each, until the marshmallows are just melted and smooth. Stir in 5 cups of the powdered sugar.

2 Grease a work surface with some of the vegetable shortening. Turn out the dough onto the greased surface. Grease your hands and knead the dough, working in enough of the remaining 3 cups powdered sugar to make a smooth, thick dough. The dough should hold the shape of a ball but still be workable. Divide the dough into 4 equal portions. Tint each portion with the red, blue, pink, and orange food coloring. Wrap the fondant in plastic wrap and let stand for a few hours to cool and firm up.

3 **Make the frosting:** In a medium bowl, beat the butter with an electric mixer on medium. Add the powdered sugar gradually. Beat in the vanilla and milk.

4 **Make the cake balls:** In a large bowl, crumble the prepared cake with your hands into fine crumbles. Add about one-fourth of the frosting; stir to combine. Gradually stir in more frosting until the cake holds together and can be shaped into balls. Scoop about 2 tablespoons of cake with a cookie scoop and roll into a 1½-inch ball. Repeat with the remaining mixture. Place the balls on a parchment-lined baking sheet. Freeze the balls for 10 minutes.

5 Place about ¼ cup of the melting wafers in a microwave-safe bowl. Microwave for about 30 seconds or until melted. Dip the end of a cake pop stick into the melted chocolate, then insert straight down into a partially frozen cake ball. (This helps "glue" the stick to the cake.) Repeat with the remaining cake balls; chill until READY to dip.

6 Before dipping the cake balls, roll out the fondant. Sift some powdered sugar onto a work surface. Roll out one portion of fondant to ¼ inch thick. Use more powdered sugar as needed when rolling to keep the fondant from sticking to the surface and the rolling pin. Cut into 2½-inch circles with a cookie cutter. Set aside and repeat with the remaining fondant portions.

7 Place the remaining melting wafers in a microwave-safe bowl. Microwave on high for 1 minute; stir. Microwave in 30-second intervals, stirring after each, until the chocolate is melted. Prepare a place to stand up the sticks after dipping. (Foam blocks work best.)

8 Dip a cake pop into the melted chocolate or spoon chocolate over the pop to cover, allowing excess chocolate to drip off. Before the chocolate sets up, drape a fondant circle over the top, letting the edges of the fondant circle hang down like a GHOST. Insert the bottom of the stick into the foam block to hold up the cake pop. Repeat with the remaining cake balls. Decorate the cake balls with candy eyes, attaching them with a tiny toothpick dab of frosting.

CHERRY POCKET PIES

Mid-Level
V
Active Time: 1 hour 30 minutes
Total Time: 1 hour 45 minutes
Makes 10 hand pies

Eat 70 PAC-DOTS and you'll be rewarded with these delightful CHERRY-filled hand pies. Eat another 170 PAC-DOTS and you'll get another one! Be careful, though—if you don't take your first bite within 10 seconds after they appear, they'll vanish.

FOR THE PASTRY

2½ cups all-purpose flour, plus more for kneading

1 teaspoon salt

¾ cup unsalted butter, cut into slices

½ to ⅔ cup cold water

FOR THE FILLING

⅔ cup sugar

1½ tablespoons cornstarch

3 cups fresh pitted or frozen tart CHERRIES, thawed

½ teaspoon almond or vanilla extract

FOR THE EGG WASH

3 egg yolks, divided

3 teaspoons water, divided

Red and green gel paste food coloring

4 ounces marzipan

Brown gel paste food coloring

1 Make the pastry: Place the flour and salt in the bowl of a food processor. Process briefly to combine. Add the butter slices; pulse until the butter is the size of peas. Add the cold water, 2 tablespoons at a time, processing just until combined after each addition. Add enough water to make a dough that holds together and will form a ball. Divide the ball in half. Wrap in plastic wrap and chill for 30 minutes or up to 4 hours.

2 Make the filling: In a medium saucepan over medium heat, combine the sugar and cornstarch. Add the CHERRIES; cook, stirring, until the CHERRIES release their juice and the mixture becomes thick. Cook and stir for 2 minutes longer. Remove from the heat; stir in the almond extract. Fill a large bowl with water and ice cubes. Set the saucepan in the water to quickly chill the CHERRY filling, stirring occasionally.

3 Make the egg wash: In a small bowl, stir together 2 of the egg yolks and 2 teaspoons of the water. Stir in enough red food coloring to make a rich red color; set aside. In another bowl, stir together the remaining egg yolk, remaining 1 teaspoon water, and a small amount of green food coloring; set aside.

4 Preheat the oven to 375°F. Line two baking sheets with parchment paper.

5 Place one portion of dough on a lightly floured surface. Roll out the dough to ¼ to ⅛ inch thick. Cut into 4-inch circles using a large cookie cutter or a jar lid. Place the circles 1 inch apart on the prepared baking sheets. Spoon about ¼ cup chilled CHERRY filling onto the centers of the dough circles. Roll out the remaining dough and cut out more 4-inch circles. Place the circles on top of the CHERRY filling; press the edges of the dough with a fork to seal. Cut 1½-inch leaf shapes from dough scraps; set aside.

6 Using clean artists paintbrushes, brush the filled pastries with the red egg wash mixture. Brush the leaves with the green egg wash mixture. Bake until the pastry is flaky and the edges just begin to brown (8 to 10 minutes for leaves, 15 to 20 minutes for pies). Let cool on a wire rack.

7 To serve, lightly tint marzipan with brown gel paste food coloring. Divide into 10 equal pieces and roll into skinny ropes to create the stems. Arrange pocket pies, stems, and leaves on a serving platter.

ORANGE SORBET

Mid-Level
V+, GF, DF
Active Time: 30 minutes
Total Time: 2 hours 30 minutes
Makes 6 servings

Take 500 points for the win with this whimsical and refreshing sorbet that's a spitting image of the juiciest of the FRUITS. Pick the roundest ORANGES you can find to give the serving vessels the most "a-peeling" shape.

6 navel ORANGES

⅓ cup sugar

2 tablespoons water

6 fresh mint leaves, plus more for garnish

¼ teaspoon vanilla extract (optional)

1 Cut the ORANGES in half. Use a citrus reamer to juice the ORANGES to yield 2 cups, reserving six of the ORANGE skin shells to use later for serving. Use a spoon to scrape any remaining loose pulp from the insides of the shells. Freeze the ORANGE shells.

2 In a medium microwave-safe bowl, combine the sugar and water. Microwave for 30 seconds; stir to dissolve the sugar. If necessary, microwave for another 15 seconds to dissolve the sugar. Stir in the mint leaves. Let steep for 5 minutes. Remove the mint; stir in the ORANGE juice and vanilla, if using.

3 Place the mixture in an electric ice cream/sorbet maker and churn according to the manufacturer's directions. (Or place the mixture in a small freezer-safe pan. Freeze for 2 to 3 hours, stirring every 30 minutes to break up icy chunks and make a thick, slushy consistency.) Immediately after churning, spoon the sorbet into the frozen ORANGE shells, piling sorbet into a mound. Freeze the filled shells for at least 2 hours or up to 4 hours.

4 To serve, let stand at room temperature for 5 to 15 minutes to soften. Garnish with additional mint leaves just before serving.

FRUIT-FETTI CUPCAKES

Pro
V
Active Time: 3 hours
Total Time: 3 hours
Makes 20 cupcakes

Picking up one of these fantastic FRUIT-topped cupcakes is easier than picking up points, but both things are pretty sweet! Marzipan—sweetened almond paste—is easy to work with, delivers WOW-factor results, and is really tasty too.

Special equipment: 4 small bowls and 4 small clean artists brushes

FOR THE MARZIPAN FRUITS

Powdered sugar, for dusting

One 7- to 8-ounce package marzipan

Red, orange, and brown gel food coloring

1 egg white, lightly beaten

6 teaspoons water, divided

Red sanding sugar

Fresh rosemary sprigs

Whole cloves

Corn syrup, for brushing

FOR THE CUPCAKES

2½ cups sifted cake flour or all-purpose flour

1 tablespoon baking powder

½ teaspoon salt

4 large egg whites, lightly beaten

1 cup whole milk

10 tablespoons unsalted butter, softened

1⅓ cups granulated sugar

2 teaspoons clear vanilla extract or regular vanilla extract

⅔ cup multicolor oblong sprinkles

FOR THE FROSTING

One 8-ounce package cream cheese, softened

½ cup unsalted butter, softened

2 teaspoons clear vanilla extract or regular vanilla extract

5 to 6 cups sifted powdered sugar

1 **Make the marzipan FRUITS:** Dust a work surface with a little powdered sugar. Knead the marzipan with your hands on the surface to soften. If the marzipan is dry, knead in a few drops of water. Divide into four portions. Tint two portions with the red food coloring. Tint one of the portions with the orange food coloring. Tint the last portion dark red using the red and brown food coloring. Keep the marzipan covered with plastic wrap when not shaping. Place the egg white in a small bowl. Place a couple drops of red food coloring in a small bowl and stir in 2 teaspoons of the water. Do the same with the orange and brown food coloring. Place the sanding sugar in another bowl.

2 For STRAWBERRIES, shape one red portion of marzipan into five balls. Roll the balls in your hands to form into a STRAWBERRY shape. Brush with some egg white. Roll the STRAWBERRIES in some red sugar. Cut a piece of rosemary sprig so it has only one row of leaves and about ½ inch of woody stem. Trim the leaves and stick the sprig into the top end of the STRAWBERRY for the stem; set aside.

3 For APPLES, divide the second red portion of marzipan into five balls. Flatten the top and bottom of the balls, and use the end of a brush to make a little indentation on the top of the balls. Brush with a little red food coloring. Place a whole clove at the top of each APPLE for the stem; set aside.

4 For ORANGES, divide the orange portion of marzipan into five balls. Roll the balls over a metal grater to make texture. Brush the ORANGES all over with egg white. Remove the ball end of a whole clove and stick the remaining piece of the clove into the top of the ORANGE for a stem; set aside.

Recipe continues on next page . . .

146

5 For CHERRIES, divide the dark red portion of marzipan into 10 smaller balls. Make an indentation on top of the CHERRIES with the end of brush handle. Brush the CHERRIES with some corn syrup. Add a single rosemary leaf to the top of each CHERRY for a stem; set aside.

6 **Make the cupcakes:** Preheat the oven to 350°F. Line 20 standard muffin cups with cupcake liners; set aside.

7 In a medium bowl, whisk together the cake flour, baking powder, and salt; set aside. In another bowl, whisk together the egg whites and milk; set aside.

8 In a large mixing bowl, beat the butter on medium speed for 30 seconds. With the mixer on medium-high speed, gradually add the granulated sugar, scraping the sides of the bowl occasionally. After combined, beat for another 2 minutes until fluffy. Beat in the vanilla.

9 Add the flour mixture and the milk mixture alternately in batches, beating on low speed after each addition until combined. Scrape the sides of the bowl and beat on medium speed for another 30 seconds. Stir in the sprinkles. Divide the batter evenly among the cupcake liners, filling them two-thirds full. Bake until a toothpick inserted into center of a cake comes out clean, 15 to 20 minutes. Let cool in the pans on a wire rack.

10 **Make the frosting:** In a large mixing bowl, beat the cream cheese with an electric mixer on medium speed until soft and creamy. Beat in the butter and vanilla until smooth. Gradually beat in the powdered sugar. Beat on high speed for 3 minutes until fluffy. Place the frosting in a large piping bag with an extra-large star piping tip.

11 Remove the cooled cupcakes from the pan. Pipe swirls of frosting on each cupcake and add sprinkles. Top with a single marzipan FRUIT or two CHERRIES.

SUPERCOOL PAC-MAN MINTS

Beginner
V, GF
Active Time: 1 hour
Total Time: 2 hours
Makes about 20 mint patties

Freshen up your PAC-MAN moves with these chocolate-covered, melt-in-your-mouth mint patties. The invigorating flavor of mint will help you keep your cool through even the most treacherous moments navigating the perils of the MAZE.

⅓ cup unsalted butter, softened

⅓ cup light corn syrup

8 drops peppermint oil or
1 teaspoon peppermint extract

4 cups sifted powdered sugar

One 10-ounce package dark chocolate melting disks

1 tablespoon vegetable shortening

Sprinkles in PAC-MAN colors
(blue, yellow, pink, red, orange)

1 Line two baking sheets with parchment paper.

2 In a medium mixing bowl, beat the butter with an electric mixer until creamy. Beat in the corn syrup and peppermint oil. Gradually add the powdered sugar, 1 cup at a time. Beat until well combined and smooth. Portion the mixture into 1-inch balls with a small cookie scoop. Roll into balls and place 2 inches apart on one of the prepared baking sheets. Place a second sheet of parchment on top. Flatten the balls with the bottom of a drinking glass to ¼ to ½ inch thick. Freeze for 30 minutes.

3 Place the melting disks and vegetable shortening in a heatproof bowl set over a pan of simmering water. Stir with a rubber spatula until melted and smooth. Decrease the heat and keep the chocolate warm.

4 Remove the patties from the freezer and peel off the top parchment sheet. Stick a fork into a patty and quickly dip into the melted chocolate. Wipe the excess chocolate off the bottom of the patty on the edge of the bowl. Transfer the dipped patty to the second prepared baking sheet. Add a few sprinkles while the chocolate is still wet. Repeat with the remaining patties. Chill the dipped patties for 30 minutes or until the chocolate is hardened. Peel the patties off the parchment paper when the chocolate has hardened. Store the patties in the refrigerator.

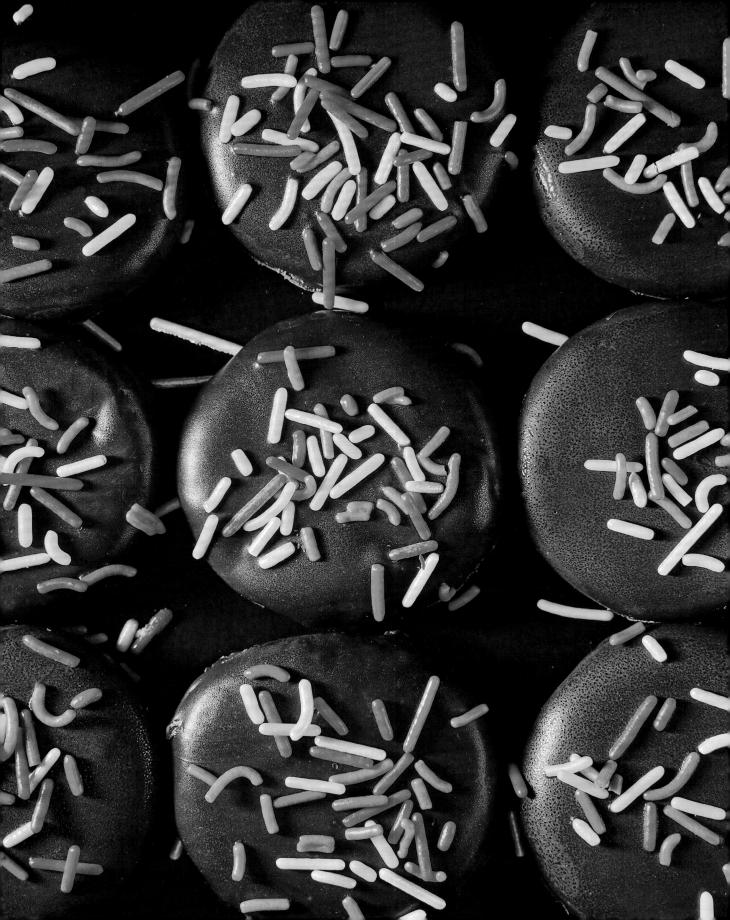

A-MAZE-ING PAC-MAN PARTY CAKE

Pro
V
Active Time: 3 hours
Total Time: 4 hours
Makes 12 servings

When it's PAC-MAN party time, this jaw-dropping cake is the way to play! Use customized cookie cutters or the patterns provided on page 158 to create the character shapes. An easy homemade marshmallow fondant ensures that it will be fresh, soft, and easy to work with.

SPECIAL EQUIPMENT

¼-, ½-, ¾-, and 1 ¼-inch round fondant or clay cutters

FOR THE MARSHMALLOW FONDANT

One 16-ounce package mini marshmallows

2 tablespoons water

8 cups sifted powdered sugar, plus more for rolling, divided

¼ cup vegetable shortening

Gel paste food coloring (PAC-MAN colors of black, yellow, blue, red, pink, peach, and orange)

FOR THE POLKA-DOT CAKE BALLS

One 18-ounce white cake mix, batter prepared according to package directions, unbaked

Yellow, blue, peach, pink, and orange gel paste food coloring

5 ounces white chocolate, melted

Vegetable shortening

1 **Make the marshmallow fondant:** Place the marshmallows and water in a large microwave-safe bowl. Microwave on high for 1 minute; stir. Microwave in 30-second increments, stirring after each, until the marshmallows are just melted and smooth. Stir in 5 cups of the powdered sugar. Grease a work surface with some of the vegetable shortening. Turn out the dough onto the greased surface. Grease your hands and knead dough, working in enough of the remaining 3 cups powdered sugar, to make a smooth, thick dough. The dough should hold the shape of a ball but still be workable. Set aside one-fourth of the fondant dough. Tint the remaining three-fourths of the fondant dough with enough black food coloring to make a deep color. Knead the food coloring into the dough until uniform in color. Wrap in plastic wrap and set aside. (It helps to wear kitchen gloves to prevent staining when working with black food coloring.) Divide the reserved dough into six portions. Tint each portion different PAC-MAN colors with yellow, blue, red, peach, pink, and orange food coloring, kneading the dough to combine. Wrap the colored fondants in plastic wrap and let stand for a few hours to cool and firm up.

2 **Make the polka-dot cake balls:** Preheat the oven to 350°F. Grease five 8-by-4-inch loaf pans. (If you don't have enough loaf pans, you can bake in batches.) Line two or three baking sheets with parchment paper.

3 Divide the white cake batter evenly among five bowls. Tint each portion as desired using the yellow, blue, peach, pink, and orange food coloring. Pour each color of batter into a prepared loaf pan. Bake until a toothpick inserted into the center comes out clean, about 15 minutes. Remove from the pans and cool completely.

4 Trim any browned crusts from the colored cakes and discard. Finely crumble each color of cake into separate bowls. Add 1 ounce of melted white chocolate to each of the bowls. Stir to combine the cake crumbs and melted chocolate. Measure 1 tablespoon of the crumb mixture for each ball. Grease your hands with vegetable shortening and roll the mixture into a 1-inch ball. Place on the prepared baking sheet. Repeat with all the cake colors. Chill until firm, about 30 minutes.

Recipe continues on next page . . .

FOR THE LARGE CAKE

6 egg whites

3 cups all-purpose flour

1½ teaspoons baking powder

¾ teaspoon baking soda

¾ teaspoon salt

¾ cup unsalted butter, softened

3 cups granulated sugar

2 cups buttermilk

1 teaspoon vanilla extract

1 teaspoon almond extract

FOR DECORATING

2 cups prepared creamy white frosting

Royal blue gel paste food coloring

Dark blue edible marker

½-inch candy eyeballs

5 **Make the large cake:** Let the egg whites stand at room temperature for 30 minutes. Grease a 9-by-13-inch baking pan. Line the bottom of the pan with parchment paper. Grease the parchment; dust pan with flour. Set aside. Preheat the oven to 350°F.

6 In a large bowl, whisk together the flour, baking powder, baking soda, and salt.

7 In the bowl of a stand mixer fitted with the paddle attachment, beat the butter for 30 seconds. With the mixer on medium-high speed, gradually add the granulated sugar. Scrape the sides of the bowl and beat until very fluffy, about 3 minutes. Add the egg whites a little at a time, beating well after each addition. Alternately beat in the flour and buttermilk, beating after each addition until combined. Beat in the vanilla and almond extracts. Scrape the bowl and beat to combine well. Pour half of the batter into the prepared baking pan. Drop the chilled cake balls into the batter, arranging them evenly throughout the batter. Top with remaining batter.

8 Bake until a toothpick inserted into the center of the cake comes out clean, 40 to 45 minutes. Let cool in the pan on a wire rack until completely cooled. Loosen the edges of the cake from the pan. Carefully invert onto a serving platter, discarding the parchment paper.

9 **Decorate the cake:** Dust a work surface lightly with powdered sugar. Use a rolling pin to roll out the black portion of fondant to ¼ inch thick, roughly in a rectangular or oval shape (16 by 12 inches). Use additional powdered sugar to keep the fondant from sticking to the surface and the rolling pin. Spread 1 cup of the frosting in a thin layer over the top and sides. To transfer the sheet of black fondant to the cake, gently roll the fondant onto the rolling pin. Then, holding the rolling pin over one edge of the cake, carefully unroll the fondant, allowing it to drape over the entire cake. Press the fondant down over the sides of the cake to cover. Trim away excess fondant at the corners and bottom edges.

10 On the same work surface with the powdered sugar, roll out the colored fondants to ⅛ inch thick. Use a small cutter* or the pattern on page 158 to cut out GHOST shapes. Use a 1 ¼-inch cutter to cut out PAC-MAN. Use a small sharp knife to cut a triangle for his mouth. Use a ¾-inch cutter to cut out POWER PELLETS. Use a ¼-inch cutter to cut out PAC-DOTS. Tint remaining frosting royal blue. Place frosting in a piping bag fitted with a small round tip.

11 Pipe very thin lines of blue frosting in a MAZE pattern on cake. (*See pattern on page 158.*) Use the dark blue edible marker to cover the black pupils on the candy eyeballs and make them look up, down, left and right. Attach the candy eyeballs to GHOSTS with small dots of frosting. Attach PAC-MAN and GHOST cutouts where desired on the MAZE, using a little frosting on the backs of the cutouts. Place POWER PELLETS and PAC-DOTS in the MAZE as desired.

*Tip: Customizable cookie cutters are available online. If you don't want to purchase a cutter or fondant cutters, use the patterns on page 158 to cut out GHOST, PAC-MAN, PAC-DOT, and POWER PELLET shapes from a piece of paper. Lay the patterns on the rolled-out fondant and use a small sharp knife to cut around them.

500-POINT CREAMSICLE POPS

Beginner
V, GF
Active Time: 15 minutes
Total Time: 4 hours 45 minutes
Makes 10 pops

Lick your ghostly foes, then take a break from the action with these refreshing freezer pops of ORANGE and vanilla bases swirled together for a cool, creamy treat. ORANGE and vanilla are a CLASSIC flavor dream team.

FOR THE ORANGE BASE

One 12-ounce container frozen ORANGE juice concentrate

¼ cup heavy cream

¾ cup water

FOR THE VANILLA BASE

Two 6-ounce containers whole milk plain yogurt

½ cup heavy cream

¼ cup sugar

2 teaspoons vanilla extract

Pinch of salt

1 Make the ORANGE base: In a blender, combine the ORANGE juice concentrate, cream, and water. Cover and blend until smooth.

2 Make the vanilla base: In a small bowl, whisk together the yogurt, cream, sugar, vanilla, and salt until smooth.

3 Use a spoon (or a funnel) to alternate adding the ORANGE base and the vanilla base to each of 10 silicone ice pop molds. Use a bamboo skewer or a toothpick to swirl the ORANGE and vanilla. Freeze for 30 minutes. Insert pop sticks into the molds and freeze for 4 hours.

ABOUT THE AUTHORS

Lisa Kingsley has more than 30 years' experience as a food writer, editor, and recipe developer. Her work has appeared in magazines such as *Fine Cooking* and *Better Homes & Gardens*. She collaborated with the *Smithsonian Institution on American Table: The Foods, People, and Innovations That Feed Us* (Harvest, 2023). She is the coauthor of *Cooking with Magic: A Century of Recipes Inspired by Disney's Animated Films from Steamboat Willie to Wish* (Insight Editions, 2023) and *The Powerpuff Girls: The Official Cookbook* (Insight Editions, 2024). She has fond memories of playing PAC-MAN and eating awesome snacks with her friends in the 1980s at the arcade in Mason City, Iowa.

Jennifer Peterson has been food styling and developing recipes for cookbooks and magazines for more than twenty-five years. She has styled covers for *Better Homes & Gardens* magazine and styled *Emily in Paris: The Official Cookbook* (Insight Editions, 2022), *Star Wars Galactic Baking: The Official Cookbook of Sweet and Savory Treats from Tatooine, Hoth, and Beyond* (Insight Editions, 2021), *Disney Princess Tea Parties Cookbook* (Insight Editions, 2022), and *Disney Villains: Devilishly Delicious Cookbook* (Insight Editions, 2022). She coauthored and styled *Cooking with Magic: A Century of Recipes Inspired by Disney's Animated Films from Steamboat Willie to Wish* (Insight Editions, 2023). Jennifer is a 1980s girl who enjoyed playing CLASSIC video games like PAC-MAN.

Tricia Bergman is a food scientist, food editor, recipe developer, and test kitchen professional employed in the creative world of food for more than 30 years. She enjoys the variety of her work, which includes contributions to *The Real Paleo Diet* (Harvest, 2015), *It's a Wonderful Life: The Official Bailey Family Cookbook* (Insight Editions, 2021), and *The Powerpuff Girls: The Official Cookbook* (Insight Editions, 2024), to name just a few. PAC-MAN came out her freshman year in college, and she has fond memories of playing with friends in the student union—it was THE thing to do in college!

MAZE WALLS

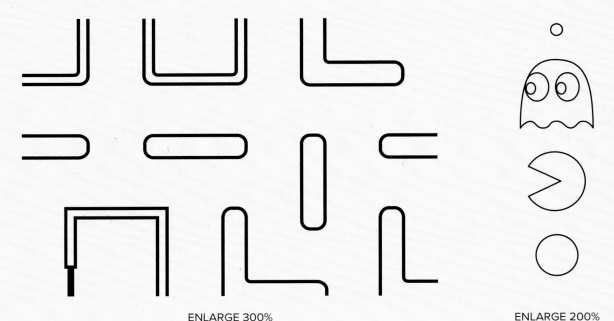

ENLARGE 300%

ENLARGE 200%

CONVERSION TABLES

KITCHEN MEASUREMENTS

CUP	TABLESPOON	TEASPOON	FLUID OUNCES
$\frac{1}{16}$ cup	1 tablespoon	3 teaspoons	$\frac{1}{2}$ fluid ounce
$\frac{1}{8}$ cup	2 tablespoons	6 teaspoons	1 fluid ounce
$\frac{1}{4}$ cup	4 tablespoons	12 teaspoons	2 fluid ounces
$\frac{1}{3}$ cup	$5\frac{1}{3}$ tablespoons	16 teaspoons	$2\frac{2}{3}$ fluid ounces
$\frac{1}{2}$ cup	8 tablespoons	24 teaspoons	4 fluid ounces
$\frac{2}{3}$ cup	$10\frac{2}{3}$ tablespoons	32 teaspoons	$5\frac{1}{3}$ fluid ounces
$\frac{3}{4}$ cup	12 tablespoons	36 teaspoons	6 fluid ounces
1 cup	16 tablespoons	48 teaspoons	8 fluid ounces

GALLON	QUART	PINT	CUP	FLUID OUNCES
$\frac{1}{16}$ gallon	$\frac{1}{4}$ quart	$\frac{1}{2}$ pint	1 cup	8 fluid ounces
$\frac{1}{8}$ gallon	$\frac{1}{2}$ quart	1 pint	2 cups	16 fluid ounces
$\frac{1}{4}$ gallon	1 quart	2 pints	4 cups	32 fluid ounces
$\frac{1}{2}$ gallon	2 quarts	4 pints	8 cups	64 fluid ounces
1 gallon	4 quarts	8 pints	16 cups	128 fluid ounces

OVEN TEMPERATURES

CELSIUS	FAHRENHEIT
93°C	200°F
107°C	225°F
121°C	250°F
135°C	275°F
149°C	300°F
163°C	325°F
177°C	350°F
191°C	375°F
204°C	400°F
218°C	425°F
232°C	450°F

WEIGHT

GRAMS	OUNCES
14 grams	$\frac{1}{2}$ ounce
28 grams	1 ounce
57 grams	2 ounces
85 grams	3 ounces
113 grams	4 ounces
142 grams	5 ounces
170 grams	6 ounces
283 grams	10 ounces
397 grams	14 ounces
454 grams	16 ounces
907 grams	32 ounces

LENGTH

IMPERIAL	METRIC
1 inch	$2\frac{1}{2}$ centimeters
2 inches	5 centimeters
3 inches	10 centimeters
4 inches	15 centimeters
6 inches	20 centimeters
8 inches	25 centimeters
12 inches	30 centimeters

INSIGHT
EDITIONS

PO Box 3088
San Rafael, CA 94912
www.insighteditions.com

Find us on Facebook: www.facebook.com/InsightEditions
Follow us on Instagram: @insighteditions

ISBN: 979-8-88663-751-9

Publisher: Raoul Goff
SVP, Co-Publisher: Vanessa Lopez
Publishing Director: Mike Degler
VP, Creative: Chrissy Kwasnik
VP, Manufacturing: Alix Nicholaeff
Executive Editor: Jennifer Sims
Senior Editor: Eric Geron
Managing Editor: Nora Milman
Production Manager: Deena Hashem
Strategic Production Planner: Lina s Palma-Temena

Recipes by Lisa Kingsley, Jennifer Peterson, and Tricia Bergman, Waterbury Publications, Inc.
Written by Lisa Kingsley, Waterbury Publications, Inc.
Photography by Ken Carlson, Waterbury Publications, Inc.
Food Styling by Jennifer Peterson, Waterbury Publications, Inc.

ROOTS of PEACE   REPLANTED PAPER

Insight Editions, in association with Roots of Peace, will plant two trees for each tree used in the manufacturing of this book. Roots of Peace is an internationally renowned humanitarian organization dedicated to eradicating land mines worldwide and converting war-torn lands into productive farms and wildlife habitats. Roots of Peace will plant 2 million fruit and nut trees in Afghanistan and provide farmers there with the skills and support necessary for sustainable land use.

Manufactured in China by Insight Editions
10 9 8 7 6 5 4 3 2 1